RESOLVING Conflict ONCE & FOR ALL

A Practical How-To Guide to Mediating Disputes

by Mark Stein
with Dennis J. Ernst

**Harmony House
Publishers Louisville**

Resolving Conflict Once and For All
Published jointly by Harmony House Publishers and
Mediation First
101Crescent
Louisville, KY 40206
phone: (502) 897-3020
fax: (502) 899-1545

Harmony House
(502) 228-2010

All rights reserved. No part of this book may be reproduced or transmitted in any form or by any means, electronic or mechanical, including photocopying, recording or by any information storage and retrieval system without written permission from the authors, except for the inclusion of brief quotations in a review.

Copyright © 1997 by Mark Stein and Dennis J. Ernst
ISBN 0-9656429-0-9

Table of Contents

Foreword
Introduction   v

Section 1:
An Introduction To Mediation

The Necessity for Mediation   2
What is mediation?   7
Disputes anyone can mediate   9
The risks of not mediating   11

Conflict Pathways   18
Alternatives to mediation   18
Mentalities that resist mediation   19
How conflicts come to mediation   21

Section 2:
Conducting The Mediation Session

Opening Remarks   26
Step 1: Welcome and introduction   28
Step 2: Voluntary nature of mediation   28
Step 3: Your role as mediator   28
Step 4: Agreement on ground rules   29
Step 5: Review the agenda   33

Exploring Facts and Feelings   34
Step 6: Getting the facts   34
Step 7: Question and response   34
Step 8: Exploring feelings   42

Resolution 46
Step 9: The agreement 46
Step 10: Addressing future conflicts 52
Step 11: Drafting the resolution 54
Summarizing the steps 56

Section 3:
The Dynamics Of Mediation

Creating a Favorable Mediation Environment 59
Mediation models 59
Location 60
Lighting 61
Color 61
The great table debate 62
Body language 63
Seating orientation 64
The qualities of a successful mediator 66

Surviving Deadlocks, Tension and Allies 70
When mediation fails 70
High tension disputes 74
Witnesses 76
Support persons 77
Attorneys 80

Advanced Mediation 83
Perspective through visualization 83
The power of agreement 87

Section 4:
Applications For Mediation

Mediation in the Work Place   91
Installing a mediation policy in the work place   91
Using an internal mediator   94
What to look for in an internal mediator   95
Using an external mediator   96
What to look for in an external mediator   100
Record keeping   101

Mediation in Schools   102
Internal mediation   103
Installing internal mediation   104
Community mediator support   105
Establishing the mediation protocol   105
Student mediator selection   106
Communication   106
Record keeping   107
External mediation   108

Other Applications   109
Mediation for therapists   109
Attorneys and mediation   112
    Attorneys as mediators   114
    Attorneys referring conflicts to mediation   116
Victim/offender mediation   116
Other applications   118
    Divorce cases   118
    Disputes against healthcare providers   118

Commercial disputes	119
Personal injury/property damage	119
Franchise disputes	120
Business partnerships	121
Product liability	123
Securities industry	123

The Future of Mediation 123
Real estate transactions 124
Prenuptial agreements 127

Appendix I 130
Consent and Confidentiality Agreement 130

Appendix II 131
Items of Agreement 131

Appendix III 132
Sample Agreements 132

Appendix IV 133
Resources 134

Foreword

Increasing diversity, rapid change and the dawning global information age increasingly influence our everyday lives. Developing strong skills to interact more effectively with other people is becoming ever more vital to achieve both personal and career success. With *Resolving Conflict Once and For All,* consultant and author Mark Stein provides timely, practical and well-focused tools to meet this need.

Based on his experience in mediating more than a thousand disputes, his personal philosophy of win-win solutions to seemingly impossible problems and his well-developed sense of perspective and humor can benefit anyone with a sincere desire to facilitate more productive relationships between people. The tools and techniques presented should be part of the basic skills of everyone who deals with others—in the professions, in business and personal relationships, and in everyday life.

Resolving Conflict Once and For All is not only easily readable and delightfully entertaining, but is also a step-by-step training manual to empower readers to help both individuals and groups develop productive and satisfying patterns of interacting. From the workplace to schools to consumer problems to personal relationships, the scope of the book is broad and the methods are powerful. Beginning with a definition of what mediation is all about, Stein takes the reader on a journey through the entire mediation process in a logical progression that is both easy to understand and to apply.

The approach is "hands on" and can be used in a surprisingly wide variety of situations. Illustrative anecdotes are cleverly woven into the text to reinforce the lessons being learned. Topics are covered thoroughly and logically, even including such tips as how to choose the best surroundings and effectively read body language. A helpful Appendix provides sample documents such as a consent agreement which can be extremely useful to a beginning mediator.

This book, clearly written from the heart yet with an applied "real world" focus, should have great appeal to all readers interested in self-improvement and developing practical skills to increase the productivity, well-being and satisfaction of those around them. The author well equips and launches beginning mediators on a worthwhile journey that can lead to a lifetime of enrichment both for themselves and all the people that they have the skills to help.

Gerald D. Ramsey, Ph.D., Associate Professor of Business Administration, Division of Business and Economics, Indiana University (Southeast)

Introduction

Mediation has a glorious quality about it that separates it from every other alternative dispute resolution technique: *the process can be applied universally*. Every basic dispute, complete with whatever quirks, variations and side shows that make them however unique, can be resolved using the methods within this book regardless of the eccentricity of the conflict. You can use the same steps to resolve the scheduling dispute in your office in the morning as you can your kids' argument over who walks the dog that night.

Because mediation is such a universal procedure, my hope is that the new mediators this book creates realize that they are as equally equipped to help resolve the conflicts that arise on the fringe of their personal lives as they are those that erupt in the work place. To that end, I make two fictitious conflicts arise and come to resolution in this text: a work place dispute and a community dispute. In the process, the basic tenets of mediation will be reinforced through the two scenarios, which I've attempted to make refreshingly diverse.

Since I must refer to disputing individuals so frequently in my discussions here, I use several terms interchangeably throughout to avoid the monotonous, repetitive, drum beat of a single term. Therefore, when I talk about conflicting individuals I refer to them as "participants," "antagonists," "adversaries," "principals," "disputants," "disparate parties," or simply "parties," fully realizing that to those in conflict, the word "party" does little to define their ordeal.

Having mediated well over a thousand disputes, I have waded through the muck of human foibles at times so bizarre and at other times so sobering that I am convinced our behavior could be best summed up by saying that it is intriguing at best, tragic at worst, rarely predictable, and seldom rational. Some of my cases have been disturbing, some hilarious; most of them have been somewhere in between. If I resort to humor too often to illustrate a point during the course of this book, I apologize. It's only because if those of us who embroil ourselves in conflicts for a living don't laugh about what we've gotten ourselves into, we'll cry. Indeed, many times I've had to remind myself that comedy is tragedy plus time.

But be they ridiculous or sublime, I have always held my disputants in high regard for possessing one highly admirable quality. In all of my successful sessions, its presence fuels my enthusiastic hope for our civilization's progress toward a more harmonious coexistence. That basic element is the human desire for the non-violent resolution of conflict. It is a quality without which we as individuals and as a society are hopelessly lost.

M.S.

Section 1:
An Introduction to Mediation

When a man fights, it means that a fool has lost his argument.
— Chinese proverb

The Necessity for Mediation

A work place dispute

It's the end of the fiscal year. You have to present your department's financial report to the CEO in two days, and two of your top sales executives have yet to turn in their figures. They were due yesterday. To make matters worse, you just got off the phone with one of your top corporate accounts who just exploded in your ear because of a missed order that will cost him thousands in retail sales.

You sense a festering animosity between Lucia and Hernandez, the executives whose reports are missing. From your office, you hear them exchanging terse remarks and slamming their telephones. You detect the souring of idle chatter throughout the department as they campaign for sympathy from the rest of the sales staff. You call them into your office and close the door.

You: *Lucia, Hernandez, what's going on?*
Lucia: *Nothing, why?*
You: *Hernandez?*
Hernandez: *Is something wrong?*
You: *To begin with, I've yet to receive the corporate sales figures from either of you. They were due yesterday. We're on the verge of losing one of our biggest corporate accounts because of a missed order, and for some reason you are both acting like children... polarizing the entire department. Do either one of you want to explain why there's so much tension between the*

two of you? Because if you don't, I'll have to find another way to explain to the CEO why my two top executives are playing catch with the biggest egg in our basket!

Hernandez: *I'm tired of taking Lucia's messages. I spend more time answering her phone than I do answering my own. She's always leaving early, taking breaks. I just can't do it any more and do my own work, too.*

Lucia: *Oh, yeah, listen to you! You've really got it bad. You don't have to worry about someone watching your kids. You just traipse off to the office leaving that pretty little wife of yours to clean up behind you, just tickled silly that she can stay home and bake cookies for your little brats! Meanwhile, you spend half your morning in the break room stuffing your face with donuts.*

Hernandez: *I don't have to take this kind of crap from you, you old crotch. I've got my share of problems, too. I just don't bring them to work and go around broadcasting them to the entire department. I have a job to do here and I make sure my personal life doesn't interfere with it.*

Lucia: *Yeah, so you have more time to screw up other people's lives. Do you know how many calls I took from your accounts last month? I could swear you're giving them my number to call if they have a problem. Meanwhile, Mr. Double Standard, I lost my baby sitter because you didn't pass along a phone message that my child was sick. Thanks a lot.*

You: *Stop it, the both of you. For cryin' out loud, I feel as if I'm the baby sitter here! Will you listen to yourselves? I haven't heard so much whining since they put the lights up at Wrigley Field. Do either of you have any idea what your squabble is doing to the company?*

Lucia: *Just tell him not to expect me to handle his accounts anymore.*

Hernandez: *And tell her to stop meddling with mine. Now if you'll excuse me, I have a report to file.*
Lucia: *There is no excuse for you!*

You are disgusted with the infantile exchange that just took place in your office. You could just let them battle it out on their own, but you know that your department's productivity will suffer even more. You foresee your employees, once a dedicated team that led the company in total sales, orienting themselves to either Lucia's or Hernandez's camp in a nightmarish deterioration of cooperation. Sales will plummet, clients will find more reliable and courteous sources for your products, you'll be forced to trim your staff and, perhaps, find yourself reassigned to Accounts Receivable, a fate worse than termination itself.

Then, when your spouse finds that she is no longer married to the head of the top corporate sales department in the city's only Fortune 500 company, she decides to leave you rather than admit to being married to someone in Accounts Receivable. Before you realize that you're better off without someone who'd rather be married to an image than a person, you humiliate yourself by begging for reconsideration. To top it all off, your newly estranged spouse takes the only thing you really cherish besides the children: the home theater system, the one with the big-screen TV that makes Arnold Schwarzenegger's nostrils look as big as sewer pipes.

A neighborhood dispute

It's October. You live in a very well-kept subdivision and you're getting your yard in shape for winter—raking the leaves, mulching the tulip bulbs, cleaning out the eaves, etc. Gradually, the voices coming from the next yard, mere background noise until now, are getting louder and growing angry in tone. You're not a nosey neighbor so you keep working. When you finally hear an

INTRODUCTION TO MEDIATION

outburst of obscenities, you stop raking and seek the source. Your neighbor, whom you've always admired for his levelheadedness, and his neighbor on the other side, a woman with a reputation for congeniality, are engaged in a heated argument. The fence is the only thing keeping them from turning each other's face into hamburger.

You know it's none of your business but you are disturbed by such a public display of temper in your otherwise tranquil neighborhood. You choose to investigate.

You: Frank, Helen, what's going on?

Frank: This overbearing wench wants me to pay her chiropractor's bill.

Helen: I wouldn't have to see the chiropractor if I hadn't been raking *your* leaves, you old goat.

Frank: They're in your yard; that makes them your leaves, lovey.

Helen: Well, they fell off of *your* tree!

Frank: Oh, I see. When it drops leaves, they're mine, but when it drops apples, they're yours. Maybe I ought to sue you for stealing my apples, Ms. Double Standard.

You (sorry you investigated but aware that it's too late to back out now): *Wait a minute. You aren't taking Frank to court over raking leaves, are you Helen?*

Helen: You damn betcha! One hundred fifty dollars for my first visit, and who knows how many more adjustments I'll need? Never would have happened if it wasn't for his leaves. I'm seeing my lawyer in the morning.

Frank: It'd be a shame if your car doesn't start again because as of right now you don't have a mechanic. S'pose you'll sue me for that, too?

You recognize (correctly) that the situation has gotten way out of hand. You can't believe these two adults, perfectly compatible neighbors until today, could be taking such a petty disagreement to the courts. You could walk away and let them follow through with their legal courses, but you know there's more at stake here than their friendship.

You foresee the entire neighborhood being pulled into the argument as households up and down the street take sides. Legendary friendships crumble; the harmony of the neighborhood unravels; parents tell their children who they can and can't have as friends. Gossip flies from mouth to ear, and litter lies from there to here. Everyone wants in on the fight. If things deteriorate further, you foresee Frank and Helen's disagreement sparking other conflicts in the neighborhood, and eventually the block takes on a neglected appearance. Personalities clash; the neighborhood block watch program becomes ineffective; street lights get shot out and strangers suddenly have shadows to spring from.

Suddenly, a most terrifying scenario seems entirely too possible: your new limited edition Elvis tumblers, the ones with a certificate of authenticity claiming that "The King" himself once actually thought about drinking from them, get stolen in a break-in. All this because you walked away this very moment when Frank and Helen's course was reversible. Like George Bailey in *It's A Wonderful Life*, you've just anticipated what the world could be like if you ran away from the problem at this pivotal juncture. As a result, you are moved to intercede; if only you knew how.

For children in this society, our at-home dispute resolution training is shabby at best. Children learn how to resolve conflict from their parents, teachers, television, peers, celebrities, governments, books, magazines, and tabloids—few of which are qualified to teach conflict resolution. Then they take those skills into adulthood and contribute to the education of the next generation.

The result: most of the methods we observe in solving everyday disputes are ineffective. Because our learned techniques don't work well, we feel awkward in resolving our conflicts and ill-equipped to help others resolve theirs. We burn bridges. We make enemies for life. We generate lingering anxiety. We hurt friends and alienate family, forever regretting how our mishandled disputes became costly—personally, financially or both.

It takes just 57 keystrokes for Hernandez to produce his sales report, and he knows all the shortcuts. But he doesn't know the key to keeping their working relationship cooperative. Likewise, it takes 15 tools to change the water pump in Helen's BMW. Frank has all of them. But he doesn't have Tool One to keep their friendship running past this bump in the road. Maybe you do. You already have one of the essentials neither parties possess: the desire to help resolve the conflict. But you don't want to solve the problem for them and you don't want to take sides. What do you do? You mediate.

What is Mediation?

Mediation is a voluntary, confidential process that allows two or more disputing parties to resolve their conflict in a mutually agreeable way with the help of a neutral third party, a mediator. Mediation should not be confused with *arbitration,* which is a process that allows a neutral person or persons to render a decision between disputing parties. Nor should it be confused with *litigation,* which is arbitration before a judge with lawyers thrown in to make it interesting . . . and expensive.

Considering all the non-violent methods to resolve conflicts—assuming that we don't resort to extortion, blackmail or international terrorism to solve our personal disputes—none of them minimize the damage and maximize our control at the same time like mediation.

Options in Conflict Resolution

threats of retaliation	win/lose
retaliation/violence	lose/lose
inaction	lose/lose
intimidation	lose/lose
litigation	win/lose
arbitration	win/lose
negotiation	win/lose or win/win
mediation	**win/win**

As a neutral third party, a mediator allows those at odds to negotiate their own settlement despite their initial inability to resolve the dispute on their own. The benefits of a mediated resolution make this option preferable to the other pathways:

- *Mediation is designed to generate win-win solutions;*
- *Mediation is inexpensive compared to litigation;*
- *Mediation keeps the control of the outcome in the hands of the disputing parties;*
- *Mediation is fast;*
- *Mediation leads to long-term solutions;*
- *Mediation is successful in 75 to 95 percent of the cases that use it.*

Mediation is not new. It's been around as long as there have been disputes, which is ever since the dawn of humanity. The first successful mediation of a dispute probably went something like this:

Ug and Og are two of the most successful hunters of the Cenozoic era. One day while hunting together, the stress of their fame works into a conflict that threatens to interrupt the food supply. Each want sole credit for their latest kill and an

INTRODUCTION TO MEDIATION

argument erupts. At risk is the evolution of the world's first intelligent species. Luckily for them and for us the world's first research anthropologist, Mook, is nearby. He sits on his haunches perplexed by the skull he has just unearthed in his latest dig. He overhears the dispute and investigates.

Ug: *My meat! I kill mastodon.*
Og: *I saw mastodon first. My meat!*
Ug: *I not kill mastodon there be no meat. Scram, old crotch.*
Og: *I not see mastodon, there be no kill. Scram, he-of-two-standards.*
Mook: *Ug, Og, others need food. Why not bury club?*
Ug: *Hmmm. Mook right. This time, why not both claim mastodon. Next hunt, Ug look, Og kill.*
Og: *Okay.*
Mook: *Great! Shake.* (Ug and Og shake hands and civilization is saved.)
Ug *(pointing to Mook's find): Say, isn't that the skull of* Homo habilis?

In today's more civilized society, community mediation is easing the burden on an increasingly overworked justice system. Since the origin of formal programs in the 1970s, over 650 community mediation programs have been established and well over 10,000 student/peer mediation programs are operating. In addition, over 120 victim-offender mediation programs exist in the U.S. whereby victims and offenders of crimes work out solutions in the form of restitution to their victims.

Disputes anyone can mediate

You don't have to be a professional to mediate disputes like Frank and Helen's, Hernandez and Lucia's or any other conflict that you might watch unfold. Regardless of your profession or education, applying the principles of dispute mediation that follow can help you to help other people resolve their conflicts before they get out of control. In the event you feel additional instruction would be of benefit, personal training is available in most metropolitan areas. (See Appendix IV for a partial listing.) But the principles included in this book are all you need to resolve most conflicts. Here are just some of the disputes that you could resolve if you were a neutral third party with the skills to mediate conflict:

- *employee/employee disputes*
- *interpersonal disputes*
- *real estate disputes*
- *simple racial discrimination claims*
- *simple human resource issues*
- *neighborhood conflicts*
- *family disagreements*
- *conflicts between children*

Under the supervision of community mediation centers, many trained individuals can mediate more complicated disputes than these. I would certainly encourage you to pursue volunteer mediation through a community center if you are so inclined to be more than an occasional mediator or to gain mediation experience to supplement this book.

Examples of disputes best mediated by professional mediation centers include:

- *employer/employee disputes*
- *merchant/customer complaints*
- *debt issues*
- *sexual harassment claims*
- *complex racial discrimination claims*

- *breach of contract*
- *complex benefits and compensation claims*
- *school-related disputes*
- *property damage*
- *auto accidents*

Certain situations, however, are not appropriate for dispute mediation even by trained community mediators. In mediation, the disagreeing parties should have a relatively equal balance of power in order to negotiate with each other as equals. In these situations this is not the case:

- *domestic violence*
- *sexual assault*
- *child assault*
- *child sexual assault*

The nature of these offenses is such that repeat violence is always possible. Placing a victim in a negotiating position with an offender can cause the victim to be victimized again—something that we all should guard against. There are some very rare and unique circumstances in which a professionally trained mediator might be able to mediate the above disputes, but this should not be attempted by anyone without extensive training.

The risks of not mediating

By all indications, the conflicts that have erupted between Lucia and Hernandez and Helen and Frank are typical of those well suited for mediated settlements. Whether or not you would be successful in bringing the parties to mediation and then to a mediated agreement depends on many factors; some are out of your control, but many aren't. We'll learn what they are and how to use them to facilitate a positive outcome. But first, let's see what happens if you choose *not* to mediate.

Work place dispute

Besides contributing to the deterioration of your department's productivity and possibly the loss of your big-screen TV, Lucia and Hernandez's dispute could proceed down several avenues:

- There is no doubt that they feel a little better having blown of some of their steam in your presence. They both know it's your job to handle anything that interferes with your staff's productivity, and they may feel some relief knowing that now it's your problem and that all they have to do is deal with the consequences.
- Now that they know that a major corporate account is threatened as a result of their spat, Lucia and Hernandez could both be feeling the impetus to clean up the dispute on their own before an axe falls, severing them from their careers. So they drift back to their job responsibilities yet fail to correct the underlying problem. They hope the problem goes away by itself, but it rarely does. Instead, grudges imbed themselves in their relationship and seek another event to ignite their tempers. Grudges are famous for generating ambivalence, and when ambivalence is the chosen path of dispute resolution, the chances for a peaceful coexistence evaporate.
- Hernandez could stop answering Lucia's telephone, in which case Lucia would stop answering Hernandez's telephone and both would be forced to operate under working conditions that don't allow for communication. By so doing, though, they forbid their lives, personal and professional, to integrate, and sit-

uations that develop at home won't be addressed at work regardless of the urgency. As a result, Hernandez can't coordinate his sales reports with Lucia's because he no longer feels comfortable with access to her records, and Lucia can't leave work to pick up her child should she become sick. Reports don't get filed on time, and Lucia goes through baby sitters like Hernandez goes through donuts. They both lose their friendship and a certain degree of personal freedom. Neither of them want that to happen, but neither of them have what it takes to resolve the dispute on their own, either.

- Lucia, on the other hand, could be bent for revenge and sabotage all of Hernandez's accounts in an attempt to get him fired . . . or transferred to Accounts Receivable. By so doing, she drags the entire department, and your career, down with her vendetta. Hernandez could do likewise.
- What you don't want to see happen is for one of your top executives to quit under the pressure of this interpersonal dispute. Both Lucia and Hernandez are quality performers and have carried your department when your other executives' sales figures were dismal. You owe your own success to their hard work, and you don't want to think about running your department without either of them. It is not only in their best interest to get through this, but in yours and in the company's as well.
- There is an outside chance that they could resolve the dispute on their own, but it seems unlikely now that the name calling has begun. It's going to depend on who's the most forgiving and who finds a protracted dispute to be too undignified to continue. Don't hold your breath.
- There is one other possible development that could put an end to the hostility and create a win-win situation. Mediation. This is where we see what kind of sales person YOU are!

Lucia is in the break room having coffee with another member of the sales staff. She hands over a typewritten letter on the company letterhead. The co-worker reads it in disbelief.

Lucia: *Wait till Hernie's wife gets this letter. I hope fat boy likes sleeping on the couch. When she reads about the affair her little sugar daddy is having, o-o-o-o-h Lordy, he'll be ducking frying pans. Maybe that obedient little wife of his will even walk out on him. Then he'll know what it's like to lose a sitter.*

Co-worker: *You can't be serious. You're not really going through with this are you? Getting even isn't like you. What's gotten into you?*

Lucia: *Honey, I'm not getting even. I'm getting ahead.*

Co-worker: *Do you know what you're losing? You probably don't know this but you and Hernandez are on track to set a new sales record this quarter. Does the word "bonus" mean anything to you? That's an extra five grand for each of you. Not if you drop this bomb, though. Work will be the furthest thing from his mind, and the bonus will be the furthest thing from your paycheck.*

Lucia: *I suppose a bonus would make life a bit easier. I sure could pay away some headaches. Oh, but sending this letter would feel so good right now.*

Co-worker: *The boss mediated one of my disputes a few years ago. It went pretty well. I'd use it again in a heartbeat. You owe it to yourself, and the rest of us, to give it a shot. What have you got to lose?*

Lucia: *Five thousand clams if I don't, I guess. Hmmm. All right, I'll try it. But you've gotta promise you never saw this letter.*

With that exchange, you see how acquaintances can steer a conflict into mediation. Upwards from 90 percent of those who have been through a mediated settlement emerge satisfied with the outcome. They become living testimonials in the community to the success of mediation.

You make your offer to mediate, and Lucia and Hernandez accept. You may just have salvaged your biggest account, your best salespersons, and possibly your own hide from the corporate meat grinder that can be activated by a poorly handled dispute. Go buy a lottery ticket; this just might be your lucky day.

Neighborhood dispute

Besides contributing to a decay in your neighborhood that results in you losing your Elvis tumblers, Frank and Helen's dispute could take any number of turns. Here are some of the possibilities for this dispute:

- The blowing off of steam might be all that Frank and Helen need in order to feel better about the situation. Having vented themselves at the expense of their friendship, not to mention a good deal of their dignity, Frank and Helen may feel that no further action is necessary except to retreat into a pattern of avoidance behavior, hoping that the problem goes away by itself. This ambivalence becomes a passive and ineffective approach to conflict resolution. As a result, since a grudge is increasingly burdensome to bear and since Helen still needs a mechanic, their avoidance behavior only stokes hard feelings that could flare up in another argument. Their grudge only perpetuates an air of hostility.
- Frank, in an act of rage, could cut down his apple tree guaranting that Helen will never have to rake leaves that fall into her yard from his tree. By so doing, he also guarantees that he will never taste Helen's famous, steaming, right-out-of-the-oven,

apple pies again, either—pies she makes for the church bake sale, one of which always finds its way to Frank's doorstep as gratitude for his mechanical favors. Because he levels his own tree, Frank becomes his own victim. They both lose their friendship and the neighborhood loses a lush green asset. It could happen.

- If Helen chooses small claims court—providing her claim doesn't exceed the maximum allowed in small claims—she's soliciting a third party to solve the problem for her. She has no control over the outcome and must accept whatever decision is handed down. Then she has to deal with a neighbor whom she's dragged into court. At best, she may be awarded reimbursement for some or all of her chiropractor's bills. At worst, the judge might laugh himself hysterical, deny her claim, and invite Frank to laugh along with him. In either case, I'll bet she loses her friend and mechanic and is restrained from ever having access to his apples again.

- Helen might think that the easiest path for her to follow is to carry out her threat and force a law suit. She could hire a lawyer to represent her in suing Frank for a financial settlement that would cover her medical expenses and, at her lawyer's urging, compensate her for those three magical words that make both of them drool for different reasons: *pain and suffering*. This forces Frank to hire his own attorney in an attempt to minimize the damage to his savings account and other assets, including his home. Their lawyers argue the case before a judge who makes a decision. Helen doesn't realize it until it's too late, but litigation took away her ability to control the outcome. It takes months if not years and exhausts her

children's inheritance as well as her weekly bingo parlay. Although it may resolve the dispute, any possibility of salvaging her friendship, the overall harmony of the neighborhood and her willing mechanic is hopelessly lost. She may win compensation for her chiropractor's bills, but she will lose many other intangibles. Better insure your tumblers. Better yet, move. This isn't going to be pretty.
- Frank and Helen could, however, resolve the dispute themselves and come up with an agreeable solution on their own. They, and any person or party at odds with another, stand a good chance of resolving the conflict to their mutual satisfaction if both actively participate in its resolution. Perhaps Frank and Helen tried and failed to negotiate a settlement before you heard the shouting, but when their tempers flared and they raised their voices the chance for a peaceful, negotiated settlement came to an abrupt halt. Their negotiations could resume, however, should they realize what's at stake and come back to each other to work it out. But knowing them as you do, you have your doubts. Frank is as stubborn as they come.
- There is, however, one other method that could turn this potentially disastrous dispute into a win-win situation. That's what *mediation* can do. And you thought that a yard was all you were going to clean up today!

We're with Helen in her lawyer's office. She's just finished explaining the case she'd like her to represent. When her attorney stops laughing under her breath, she convinces Helen that mediation is in her best interest—especially when she said that she'll either scalp one third right off the top of any award the judge might grant her or charge an hourly rate for the time she put into the case (which Helen calculates to be one third of the cash value of all her worldly possessions, or her beemer—bad water pump and all). Suddenly, your offer to mediate is looking good. With a little diplomatic elbow grease you convince Frank to join the party.

Conflict Pathways

Alternatives to mediation

It's a fact of life that often the best solutions are often the last to be considered. This maxim certainly holds true with mediation. Because of ignorance or negative attitudes, our knee-jerk reactions to offenses are often constructed to outdo the offender in an extreme of our own design and, hence, are not always in our own best interests. Before choosing a rational reaction, one that seeks a resolution rather than revenge, we explore hostile responses, ones that escalate animosities. Sometimes we come to our senses; sometimes we don't.

As we have seen with Helen and Frank and Lucia and Hernandez, all disputes follow one of several pathway, some ethical and legal, some not. Those pathways fall into these general categories:

- The parties ignore the conflict. This is often considered by one or both parties to be the easiest way to handle a dispute. The consequences of this approach however, are seldom considered and leads to the decay of relationships and self esteem. As time goes on, other unresolved conflicts are added to one's psychological workload creating a mountain of emotional baggage that influences behavior in many other areas of social interplay.
- Conflicts escalate and lead to harassment, threats, malicious or criminal behavior, violence, or even death. Anything is possible. The unthinkable happens every day.

- The disputants *negotiate*—a process by which they seek to resolve their conflict through unassisted discussions and formulate their own resolution. For those who have the wherewithal to confront each other and seek a binding resolution in good faith, mediation is not necessary. These peacemakers should not have to pay income taxes, watch commercials, clean ovens, find hair in their food, get stuck in traffic, or program a VCR. They don't deserve the agony.
- The disputants seek *arbitration,* a voluntary, court-ordered or contract-initiated process in which a neutral third party determines the resolution the parties must accept. An example of this would be small claims court. The judge hears both sides of the dispute and renders a decision to which the parties are bound. But arbitrators don't have to be judges. In some labor disputes a neutral agent familiar with the industry will hear both sides and render a legally binding decision. In either case, legal representation is optional.
- The disputants pursue *litigation* within a legal framework by which a judge or jury constructs a resolution after the claims of each disputant are presented and advanced through attorneys. They bypass mediation and become part of the legal logjam that clogs the court system. The wait drains them of their inner peace for months or years.
- The disputants *mediate,* a process in which a neutral third party assists the disputants in constructing their own mutually acceptable resolution. It's quick, inexpensive, and allows people to get on with their lives.

Mentalities that resist mediation

There are some extremely vindictive and irrational minds among us that keeps our designation as an "intelligent species" from becoming a universal truth. Certain voids in our reasoning skills produce mentalities that resist mediation:

The *you're-gonna-burn* **mentality.** In the heat of a conflict, tempers are hot. The last option even the most peace-loving individual wants to try is to work out a cooperative agreement with an antagonist. Today's society wants people and corporations to pay, and pay big.

The *a-grudge-is-a-terrible-thing-to-waste* **mentality.** Many times, unfortunately, there's more pleasure in the process than in the payoff. There seems to be joy for some in going for the jugular with little attention paid to the price they must pay to see that their concept of justice is served. Huge grudges seem almost weightless to them if they can generate enough misery. This approach however, doesn't factor in the human cost to both disputants. No matter how pleasurable, a grudge is a burden on the psyche. It's a cancer that eats away at the spirit. Bridge burners always have to be ready for a confrontation when happenstance brings them face to face with their adversary weeks, months, or years later.

The *how-was-I-supposed-to-know?* **mentality.** Surprisingly, many people still don't know that mediation exists. When the West was settled, disputes were resolved with the six shooter on Main Street at sunup. When we became civilized—make that *more* civilized—we put lawyers in our holster instead of six shooters. They've been our non-violent weapon of choice ever since. (Sadly, some still use the six shooter.)

In the 70s, along came mediation and suddenly disputants had another weapon to reach for when negotiation was not possible. Although mediation is making great progress in becoming the instrument du jour for the future conflicts, litigation—ever the American impulse—is still the trigger most people pull when a dispute arises. We've looked to the courts to determine guilt and punishment for so long that it's hard to know there's a kinder, gentler more effective device in the other holster.

Even when people overcome such negative thought processes, there is a host of other reasons why mediation is never considered. If disputants feel that their case would be easily won in a court of law, they can dump the whole mess in the hands of a lawyer. There may be so much hostility generated from the dispute that one or both of the disputants will not even consider negotiating through you with their adversary. This option is attractive only to those who have the time and money to see the case through. Lastly, disputants may have received bad legal advice from sources predisposed to litigation.

How conflicts come to mediation

Once you decide to mediate a dispute, somebody has to convince the combatants that they need you. Disparate parties often seek other avenues, which later lead them to mediation:

- *Judges who weave mediation into their sentencing;*
- *Therapists interested in the healing aspect of a mediated dispute;*
- *Insurance companies who, when named in a lawsuit, have more to lose through the courts;*
- *Human resource managers, whose job it is to find and serve their employees, not be sued by them;*
- *Acquaintances who have had their own disputes mediated successfully;*
- *Attorneys.*

More and more, I am finding that people want to avoid protracted disputes. Still, the hardest job of any mediator, be they veteran or rookie, is getting adversaries to the table. Not helping your chances is this statistic: roughly half of the disputants referred to mediation from all sources actually take advantage of the opportunity.

There is growing evidence that society's downward spiral toward negative approaches to conflict resolution is reversing. The number of people who come to me as a first rather than last resort is rising, leading me to believe that a migration away from litigation is well underway. Factors that nudge people toward mediation include:

- *the expense of litigation*
- *the anxiety that an unresolved dispute generates*
- *the threat of a physical confrontation arising from an unresolved dispute*
- *the prospect of a worsening of the dispute*
- *having the dispute become a matter of public record open to scrutiny by the tabloid-minded public*
- *the loss of control over the outcome*

In addition, unresolved employer-employee related disputes risk:

- *lost productivity*
- *loss of an otherwise valuable employee*
- *decreased employee morale in sympathetic co-workers*

When these benefits of mediation are obvious to disparate parties, enlightening them with a few well-laced truths about mediation may be all that is necessary to convince them to let you mediate. Regardless of the nature of the conflict, if you stress the following benefits to perspective participants you may make mediation their process of choice.

Mediation is fast. A joint meeting can be set up as soon as all participants' schedules permit. If the alternative to mediation is court action, you can point to a far quicker mediated resolution—days or weeks as opposed to months or years for a litigated case.

Mediation is low-cost. If you are a manager, friend or family member there may be no cost involved with mediating a dispute. Even if you are a professional mediator or you decide to bring one into your process, the highest fees charged, which may approach those of an attorney, would be split between the two parties. Whether you are helping friends, family members or co-workers, you stand to benefit from a mediated resolution as much as the disputants and would probably not charge for your time.

Mediation is very successful. Even the disputes that have the lowest probability of success are successful 75 percent of the time. Victim-offender mediation, the most successful, has a 99 percent success rate because both sides are highly motivated. In your conversations with your disputants, cite these statistics.

The more serious and unpleasant the alternative is, the more likely the disputants are to participate in a mediation session. By drawing out the alternative scenario the disputants might have to endure, mediation may look more attractive. But don't overdramatize lest you appear to be suspiciously persuasive. You want to be trusted now so that you will trusted when it counts. Don't be fooled into thinking that all people who enter into mediation do it cheerfully and agreeably. Remember, the reason they are there at all is that they are at odds over an issue that is important to them and that has generated negative feelings toward each other.

The most important point to remember when attempting to get parties to agree to mediation is that mediation should always be *voluntary*. In reality this is the only way it can be. You can force disputants to sit down in a room for an hour or so, but you cannot force them to negotiate in good faith toward resolving their dispute. Judges know this. That's why most court-ordered mediation programs limit the order to *participating in an orientation session* about mediation, not mediation itself. A few court-ordered mediation programs go further and require participants to work as much as possible toward a solution. Nudging participation in this manner gives disputants a chance to make an informed decision about the potential for mediation to help construct a resolution. The mediation process is often successful with those who are initially hesitant, assuming they are not intent on sabotaging the process.

As we have seen, the willingness to pursue mediation is directly proportional to the perceived severity of the alternative. If the consequences of not mediating are acceptable to either party, there will less likely be a mediated resolution. If, however, you can get adversaries to sit down and negotiate, the chances are very high that they will reach a lasting agreement.

Section 2:

Conducting the Mediation Session

Blessed are the peacemakers
—Matthew 5:9

Opening Remarks

Work place dispute

You've made arrangements for Lucia and Hernandez to meet with you in your office at your home. This was a wise decision. Meeting in your office at work would have introduced elements that could interfere with the process. You don't want other employees mingling around, coming and going and drawing their own conclusions about what is going on inside with the three of you. Most offices already have plenty of fodder for the gossip trough without your session adding to the feast. Holding the session in a high traffic area at work would also have generated tension, which is what you want to minimize as much as possible. Unless you have access to a remote conference room with assurances that your participants won't be seen coming and going, choose a more neutral site.

Your spouse has agreed to take the kids to the park so that you don't have any distractions or interruptions while the session is in progress. You also will not be taking any phone calls. For an hour or two *your undivided attention is paramount*. Therefore, any interruption or distraction—like when your son practices his tuba—will have a negative effect on the session.

Lucia is right on time. You escort her into your office and seat her. It's a good idea to busy yourself with something, anything that takes you away from her attention. This is important. You don't want Hernandez to suspect that you and Lucia were conversing. Even if it was totally unrelated to the dispute, it presents the image that you and Lucia already have the outcome chiseled in stone. Occupy yourself.

CONDUCTING THE MEDIATION SESSION

Fifteen minutes later, Hernandez arrives. The moment is tense but you are gracious and you seat him equidistant from you and Helen approximating a triangular orientation. (I'll explain why this alignment is critical in Section 3 under *Creating a Favorable Mediation Environment)*. The session begins.

Neighborhood dispute

You've set up an appointment with Frank and Helen to meet with you in the lounge of your office building after hours. Helen arrives right on time and you show her to her seat. Fifteen minutes later there's a knock and you welcome Frank inside. He explains that his car wouldn't start and he had to walk. He apologizes profusely. Several sarcastic remarks come to your ready wit, but you brush them all aside knowing none of them would be prudent in this context. Good call. Frank appreciates your restraint without saying as much. You seat him at a 45-degree angle and three feet away from Helen. You take the chair at the apex. The moment is tense but you temper it with a little light off-the-subject banter. The tension breaks a bit and the moment is yours to seize. You project an air of confidence, professionalism, maturity and seriousness toward the matter at hand, yet with enough informality to relax your participants.

There is saying in the Far East that trying to explain some things is like scratching your foot through your shoe. When I train mediators and supervisors in the mediation process I find that it is better to show them the process rather than tell them. I encorporate a simulated mediation session into most of my training classes. Walking through the process is better than talking through it.

Mediation is both science and art. In this walk-through we'll discuss the science of a mediation session. I've reserved my comments on the art of mediation for a later chapter. In the scenario to follow, observe, analyze, absorb and then integrate these illustrated steps into your own personal style. All you need are the basics.

Step 1: Welcome and introduction

You and the disputants are seated in circular/triangular fashion, each facing the center of the arrangement.

You: *I'd like to thank the both of you for agreeing to come into mediation. I know this isn't an easy thing to do, but I want to commend both of you for your willingness to try this process as a way to settle your dispute. I want to encourage you by saying that most people who get this far do resolve the issues they come to resolve. So you have good reason to be optimistic that you will be able to settle this matter.*

There are a number of things that I need to go over with you and ask for your cooperation on. I promise I won't talk this much during the actual process, but there are certain things I need to take care of if you will bear with me.

Both participants nod approvingly. At this point you begin to lay the foundation for the session by reiterating the nature of mediation.

Step 2: Voluntary nature of mediation

You: *Mediation is a voluntary process. Neither of you had to come here, and there is nothing you have to agree to except a few basic rules to keep things moving. If you are not able to reach an agreement there are always other options. We can discuss them if we get to that point.*

Step 3: Your role as mediator

You: *First of all I want to remind you that I am here to act as a mediator. I am not here to make a decision for you or to pass judgment. I am acting as a neutral, one who is concerned about both of you and our company (organization, school, community, etc.). My interest as a neutral person is to help the*

CONDUCTING THE MEDIATION SESSION

two of you resolve this dispute in a way that is agreeable to you both. I have no power or authority to impose a decision on you.

Step 4: Agreement on ground rules

Make sure that you have a verbal or non-verbal agreement on each of these rules before going on to the next one.

You: *Mediation is also a confidential process. I would like to ask each of you to agree that you will refrain from using anything that the other person says in this session at any future grievance hearing or court hearing that may occur if you are not able to resolve this in mediation.*

I would also ask your agreement to refrain from bringing notes, records, documents of this session, or me, your mediator, to any future grievance or court hearing that may occur if you are not able to resolve this here. This does not mean that you cannot bring up your own point of view if you need to do so. You are simply agreeing that you will not use what the other person says in this mediation session against them in the future. I have prepared a Consent and Confidentiality *form for you both to sign agreeing to this condition. Please read it and sign it if this is agreeable to you.*

I encourage you to have them agree to this in writing before continuing in the mediation session especially if there is a possibility of further court action or a grievance that might be filed. (A sample *Consent and Confidentiality* form is in the appendices.) Obviously, if this is just a dispute between family members or another informal type of mediation session, this would not be as important. However, I recall one case between a divorcing couple that underscored the importance of establishing this rule.

Both spouses brought their respective attorneys to the initial mediation session. The case was complex and bitter. Nevertheless, some progress was made in the first session. When the second session convened, the tension increased and soon the atmosphere became volatile. Finally, the wife exploded. Incensed, she released an offensive verbal barrage, stormed toward the door, turned, and said to her estranged husband, "You'd better come to court with both barrels loaded, buddy, because I'm bringing my AK-47." She slammed the door with her attorney chasing behind. Later that day, the husband's attorney made a sworn statement that the wife threatened to bring an AK-47 into the court room.

It was obvious to me that the wife was speaking figuratively and that the husband's attorney was exploiting the statement. The husband's attorney knew full well that there was an agreement not to use anything that was said within the mediation session in a court of law but was of the opinion that the session was over when the wife got up to storm out of the room. Therefore, he contended that the threat was made outside of the boundaries of the mediation session and, therefore, was admissible into a court of law.

The question this incident asks is, *when is mediation over?* The angered wife said it was over. The attorney that wanted to exploit the remark said it was over, yet we were still in the mediation room, and I hadn't adjourned the session. Because of this case, I have modified my consent forms to reflect that the mediation session is over when all disputants leave the mediation office. I suggest you specify your definition in your consent forms as well.

Ask for agreement on the next ground rule.

You: *I would also ask you to agree to refrain from interrupting each other while the other person is speaking. I have given you each note pads and pens so that if questions or comments come up along the way that you want to bring up, you can jot* *them down and discuss them at the appropriate time. Part of my job as a mediator is to make sure that each of you gets a chance to say everything you want to say, to ask questions of each other and to respond to what the other has said.*

No rule is more essential in securing an agreement as is the "no-interruption" rule. As with the other rules, wait for a verbal or nodding agreement from both parties. A simple "I'll try" is not acceptable. Translate this to mean "I hope I won't interrupt, but I probably will." If agreement on this point is not reached, stress the importance that each person has the opportunity to speak without interruption and ask again for their agreement. Stubbornness on this issue suggests a hidden agenda. Push for agreement here and watch out for violations of it later.

Likewise, be careful not to put yourself above the rules unless you want to lose the disputants' confidence in your role as mediator. It will be tempting for you to interrupt—not to be rude or assertive, but to clarify certain points that the participants may be too upset or inarticulate to explain clearly. Whatever the reason, your interruption will break their train of thought. Instead, do as you've suggested they do: jot down your thoughts and ask for clarification at the end of that particular phase of the process.

There are, however, two justifications to your interrupting a disputant. When the disputants violate the ground rules that they've agreed upon before the session, do not hesitate to interrupt and remind them that they've violated one of the rules they themselves have pledged to uphold. The train of thought here is usually one which needs to be broken for the good of the session, and you should tactfully interrupt.

The second condition that will prompt my interruption of a disputant's train of thought is when the speaker becomes redundant. Whenever I hear the words "like I said before," I know we're running on retreads and that the statement to follow is an unnecessary waste of time. This is not an opportunity to be condescending, but a time to be tactful. I suggest phrasing your attempt to move forward like this: "Are there any facts that you *haven't* discussed already that you'd like to add." If this polite tactic fails to stop redundant participants, wait until they take a breath (fortunately, we all have to do that), then ask again if there is any other *new* material to add. The message will be clear.

You: *I would also like to ask your agreement to negotiate in good faith. What that means is that I would like you to refrain from doing or saying anything that could intentionally derail this process. Name calling, finger pointing and abusive language directed at the other party are all examples of not negotiating in good faith and are counterproductive to mediation. Is that agreeable to both of you?*

Mediating *in good faith* covers a lot of territory. It means getting your participants to agree to be civilized. Well, a little civilized anyway. Some uncivilized volume might be necessary before constructing a resolution. A formal venting during the session serves this purpose and should be tolerated to a certain degree. Your presence offers the disputants the security that their words will not provoke physical retaliation by the other party. Because of this opportunity, many disputants leave the mediation session feeling better not only because they have forged an agreement, but because you have provided them with an official podium from which to spew forth their frustrations to each other under controlled circumstances. Many times that's all people want to accomplish before they agree to settle. So if one party or the other seems less than civilized, raises his or her voice or becomes terse, let it go. It's therapeutic. So long as the exchange doesn't violate any of the ground rules, so long as it doesn't dissolve into petty personal attacks on unrelated issues, so long as they stay physically separated, and so long as nobody is packing a weapon, just observe the venting and rest assured that it will contribute to a positive outcome. When it's over, move on. If any issues come out in the exchange, jot them down as they may be what's at the root of the conflict.

Negotiating in good faith also means negotiating without a gun. It only happened to me once. A wisp of a man came into his session with a long-nosed .38 strapped onto his waist. Not being one who finds entertainment value in the drama that weaponry brings to a conflict, I politely but firmly asked that the gunslinger return the pistol to his car. He obliged and the session went on to a successful resolution. Agreement to mediate in good faith is crucial. Again, wait for a verbal or nodding agreement from both parties. This is rarely a problem.

In establishing ground rules, it's important that you literally ask their agreement on them as opposed to telling them what the rules will be. There are two very good reasons why you should frame these rules as requests rather than demands. First, if a rule is violated, reminding violators that they initially agreed to the rules is much easier than reminding them that you initially insisted they concur. Secondly, by securing voluntary agreement to the rules, disputants are more likely to honor them. The very essence of mediation is based on the principle that people are much more likely to abide by agreements to which they actively commit. Also, soliciting their agreement on the minor issues of ground rules builds momentum for their agreement on the more difficult and substantive issues of the dispute itself.

Step 5: Review the agenda
You: *The first step of the mediation process is for each of you to state the facts of the situation from your own point of view. Secondly, each of you has the opportunity to ask questions and to respond to what the other has said. The third step in the*

mediation process is for each of you to share your feelings about the situation—how you felt at the time the incident occurred as well as how you feel about it today. You might also wish to share how this is affecting your family or others.

Mediation is not to be confused with counseling or therapy. The extent to which we will be dealing with your feelings will be just to let each other know how this dispute has affected you. In mediation, we do not spend an inordinate amount of time dealing with those feelings, but it's important to let each other know the extent of your feelings in order to successfully lead you to a resolution of this dispute.

The final step in the mediation process is to attempt to find a resolution that is agreeable to both of you. Specifically, I will ask each of you what you would like to see happen or not happen in the resolution of this matter. We will list them as we go. If you reach an agreement on all items, I will write them down in the form of a memorandum of understanding. Both of you will be invited to sign it if it's agreeable to you.

I would like to thank both of you for bearing with me in this preliminary part of the mediation session. Are these steps agreeable to both of you? Do either of you have any questions about the process or my role at this point?

After answering any questions, you have completed the preliminary round. The stage is set, the ground rules are agreed upon and it's time to get down to business.

Exploring Facts and Feelings

Step 6: Getting the facts

As a neutral, it is essential that you do not choose who tells their side first. By choosing the first speaker you would be showing preference. No matter how slight or innocent, it is important that you display your neutrality in every context. Give the parties ownership of the process by asking them to steer whenever possible. What this does is empower your participants to make decisions thereby giving them ownership in the outcome, a framework for reaching their own decision. When you give this approach a high priority, the hardest part of your job is over. Let's apply this step to both conflicts.

Work place dispute
You: *Let's begin with the facts. It doesn't matter who starts. Would one of you like to begin?*

Hernandez: *Lucia started all this. Why doesn't she go first?*

You: *All right, but remember, we're not here to place blame. Lucia, would you like to start?*

Lucia: *Yeah. I had an important phone call last week from my baby sitter to tell me that Jenny, my seven-year-old, was sick and that I needed to pick her up. Hernandez conveniently forgot to give me the message. When I went to pick her up after work at the usual time, my baby sitter was furious. Jenny had vomited all over her rug and was running a temperature. The baby sitter had assumed that I deliberately ignored the message. This isn't the first time this has happened. There have been other messages, not as important but still, I didn't get them either. My baby sitter refuses to watch Jenny anymore because she thinks I'm irresponsible. She said that if I couldn't respond to an emergency situation, she's not going to continue to keep my child. I don't have anyone else to keep her. Now, thanks to Hernandez, I'm in a real bind.*

You: *Thank you. If you think of any other facts of the situation just write them down. We'll come back to you in a minute. Hernandez, what's your view of the situation?*

Hernandez: Well, I did forget to give her the message, and that was my fault. But she's always getting social phone calls, and I just forgot to write this one down. She spends a lot of time on the phone and not just on work-related business. Sometimes I get behind or interrupted because I've got to stop what I'm doing, write a note and walk it over to her desk. It's disruptive. And when she is at her desk, she talks forever to her friends when she should be helping me coordinate sales reports. Now that we share some responsibilities, the time she spends on the phone usually translates into more time that I have to spend preparing the reports. Her personal phone calls are making my job more difficult. We had a project the other day that we were supposed to finish and because of her phone calls, I had to stay late and do it myself since she had to leave on time to get her kid.

Neighborhood dispute
You: Let's begin with the facts. It doesn't really matter who starts. Would either of you like to begin?

Frank: Well, she's the one who started this thing. Why doesn't she go first?

You: Although we're not here to place blame, Helen, would you like to go first?

Helen: Frank used to pick up my leaves for me every fall. Two years ago he stopped—don't ask me why. He got a bug in his britches about something or other, I don't know. Anyway, I started raking them, and now I have a back problem that the chiropractor says will need regular adjustments. I can't afford back problems. I don't get paid when I have to leave work for that. The chiropractor said if I didn't have to rake, the pain wouldn't be so severe. The worst part is that the leaves aren't even from my tree! I think Frank should be responsible for them. He probably agrees. Why else would he have been rak-

ing them all along? Besides, when my dog makes a mess in his yard, he expects me to clean it up, and I do! And if he's not responsible for picking up his leaves, then he'll have to be responsible for the consequences when I have to do it myself."

You: *Thank you. If you think of any other facts of the situation, write them down. We'll come back to you in a minute. Frank, what's your view of the situation?*

Frank: *Sure the leaves come from my tree. But you don't see me forcing the Parton's behind me to get their leaves out of my yard, do you? Maybe if I started charging them for my raking their leaves, they'd start billing Helen for their having to rake the leaves that fall into their yard from her tree. And I don't have a bug in my britches about anything. The reason I stopped doing her leaves is that my riding mower broke down, and I can't afford to fix it. If she wasn't so concerned with herself all the time, she'd have noticed that I'm raking my own yard now, too. I'd say the bug's in her britches and she wants everybody else to have one, too.*

With that, the initial airing is over. You've been taking notes with a marker on a large flip chart or note pad for all to see. By listing the issues on a flip chart as opposed to a legal pad on your lap, your notes are kept in full view of everyone. This approach maintains that atmosphere of participant ownership, which is critical to the process. With both participants observing your schematic, they can keep you from making erroneous notes. By using flip charts, once the issues are verbalized they stay out in the open facilitating a problem-solving atmosphere. Flip charts may be initially uncomfortable for you as the mediator, but I would strongly suggest that you experiment with them in light of their obvious contributions to the process. You will find them essential in untangling conflicts that are cluttered with numerous items that camouflage the real issue. No need to buy an easel, a fancy pointer, or any other elaborate paraphernalia that would emulate a board room presentation to Fortune 500 executives. A simple, inexpensive, tripod-type or cardboard table-top flip chart available at most office supply stores will suffice.

Flip charts are great for generalizing, and generalizing is great for reframing disputes. For example, if a disputant claims that the respondent called her an SOB, you can write down "name calling" on your flip chart. This may be civilizing the uncivilized but you're reframing inflammatory language into more neutral terms. As you become more experienced you will have an entire repertoire of phrases you can use to generalize behavior and streamline the issues into categories that can be easier to interpret. Some of these phrases are worked into a sample of an *Items of Agreement* form in the appendices. It would be good to familiarize yourself with them before your first case.

A top-to-bottom listing of the issues as they are raised is preferable to a side-by-side listing separated by a line down the middle. Listing one person's issues versus the other's is an antagonistic approach and could add an adversarial element to the session.

If the facts as presented by the disputants do not agree, all is not lost. Everyone is different. Two people can look at the same situation and come to totally different conclusions based on their unique perspectives. The important point for you to remember is this: *The disputants can still reach a resolution even if there is no agreement on the facts.* Simply realize when it is pointless to argue about the validity of a fact in dispute and move ahead. Explain to the disputants that it's natural and normal for people to disagree, that any disagreement on the facts will have to remain, and that they will have to accept their disagreement on that particular issue in order to move forward. Mediation is not about ferreting out the truth, it's about getting beyond conflicting perceptions of the truth for the sake of a resolution.

CONDUCTING THE MEDIATION SESSION

Step 7: Question and response

Next, allow both parties to ask questions of each other and to respond to those questions. It's important to continue in the same order in which the session began in an effort to maintain your neutrality and to contribute to the sense of order in the process. A formulaic session encourages the disputants to expect your formula, your equation, will have a logical outcome. Mediators sweat the details. This may seem to be a minor point, but any variation from a routine could be interpreted as favoritism or a disorganized format, and if anybody's going to derail this process it had better not be you.

Work place dispute

You: *Lucia, do you have any questions for Hernandez or things that you would like to respond to that he has said?*

Lucia: *Don't you realize that if my baby sitter calls it must be of some importance? Something that should be relayed?*

Hernandez: *I was busy. I meant to write it down, but right after I hung up I got a call about a missing shipment, and your message just slipped away. If I had not been thrown into another mess, I would have followed through. Then, when I thought of how many personal calls you get, I didn't think it could have been too important. At the time, I was pretty fed up with answering your phone because you hadn't been at your desk most of that morning.*

Lucia: *You have children. Don't you know how difficult it is to find a good baby sitter?*

Hernandez: *Well, my wife stays home and takes care of our children, you know that.*

Lucia: *What about when you want to go out for dinner or to parties?*

Hernandez: *My parents live nearby. They watch them. I guess I've never really had to worry about getting a sitter.*

Lucia: *I'd like to take issue with what you said about me not pulling my weight with our joint work load. I disagree. Because I'm a single parent, I have to leave on time in order to pick up my child. I take work home sometimes because I can't stay as late as you do, so I work after Jenny goes to bed. You only see what you see me do at the office. As for my personal calls, I can't control who calls me. They have my number and they just call.*

With that, Lucia has no follow-up. You sense an ending of this initial exchange and prompt her for further discussion.

You: *Lucia, do you have any other questions or comments? Has Hernandez said anything else that you would like to respond to?*
Lucia: *I guess not.*
You: *Hernandez, are there any questions you have for Lucia? Things you would like to respond to that she has said?*
Hernandez: *Well, I know we don't have a company policy about personal phone calls, but I think it's expected that we minimize those calls. When they hamper our ability to do our jobs, then it's excessive and we need to do something about it.*

This is where you would ask any questions that you have written down during the course of their exchange. Be sure to do so in a way that does not indicate any bias on your part. You may personally feel that one person's position is silly or that another's behavior is rash, but you'd better not let them detect your persuasions. Formulate your questions carefully so as not to infer a judgmental inclination or imitate an interrogation.

Things may get heated during this phase, but that's okay as long as the ground rules remain intact. Remember, an important benefit of a mediation session is that it invites a controlled venting of frustrations. Often when anger is vented, its release facilitates healing. Just don't let the venting escalate to a point where a resolution is threatened. Maintaining adherence to the ground rules usually keeps the venting constructive in the long run.

Neighborhood dispute
You: *Helen, do you have any questions for Frank or things that you would like to respond to?*
Helen: *It's not my fault that your mower broke down. Why should I have to pay for it with my back?*
Frank: *Would you rather pay for it with your money?*
Helen: *You expect me to fix your mower?*
Frank: *Why not? You expect me to rake your leaves. I didn't mind helping you out when I could. Now I can't, and suddenly I find out that my willingness to help you with your leaves has not been appreciated, but expected. Nobody likes to be taken for granted, and that's just how I feel. In a way I'm glad my mower broke down. If it hadn't, I'd still be thinking you appreciated my help.*
Helen: *I do appreciate your help. Why do you think I bake extra pies just for you every year. If you recall, I tried to pay you once and you refused. Ever since, I've baked extra pies for you when I baked for the church picnic.*
Frank: *Oh, so I'm supposed to thank you for picking my apples and turning them into pies so that your church can canonize you? I don't think so.*
Helen: *I don't do it for personal gain and I resent the accusation. I do it because I can and because my work has helped the church continue its ministry.*
Frank: *You also do it because you have free access to the best apples in the county. How'd you like to have to buy your own*

apples from now on? I'd rather cut the tree down than to be expected to rake your leaves. That would settle this whole thing.

You: Helen, do you have anymore questions for or comments to Frank?

Helen: No, except that it would be a shame if he cut the tree down. I don't want to see that happen.

You: Okay. Frank, do you have any questions or comments for Helen?

Frank: I just don't understand how she could think the leaves that fall on her property are the responsibility of the person who owns the tree. Nobody else in the neighborhood feels that way and I'm sure a judge wouldn't either.

You: Anything else, Frank?

Frank: No.

Step 8: Exploring feelings

The facts have been stated, and the disputants have questioned each other to clarify the facts. Now it's time to find out how they really feel. If the dispute is to pivot toward a resolution, this is the part of the session where it begins to turn. Maintain your neutrality in the phrasing of your questions and you will be the facilitator of a peaceful resolution if all the other elements are in place.

To get the participants to express their feelings, I find it helpful to encourage them to relive the incident. Putting them back into the situation helps them recall the feelings they had at the time. To accomplish this, I ask leading questions that help them reveal what their feelings were about each particular aspect of the situation. I also find it helpful to visualize what I would feel if I were the disputants. This facilitates empathy, which will help you to anticipate the feelings that the disputants might be harboring, yet are reluctant to bring out. This involves a delicate dance on your part. You don't want to share how you would have felt had the incident occurred to you, but you do want to see if the disputant can share what he or she felt. There is a right way and a wrong way to negotiate this dance.

Wrong way:
You: *Lucia, if I were you, I would have felt that Hernandez was the slimiest, low-rent chiseler I'd ever met. Isn't that how you felt?*

Right way:
You: *Lucia, how did Hernandez's reaction make you feel?*

One final note about projecting yourself into other people's scenarios. It is not always possible to bring out those anticipated emotions in someone who does not share their feelings easily. I don't advise you to probe too hard if you sense that the participant considers it a violation of privacy. You can't force someone to share their feelings if they're not accustomed to doing so. The best you can do is to encourage a sharing and move on when they refuse. Also, some people will want to restate the facts or jump to the resolution instead of sharing their feelings. If they do this, gently redirect them by asking again how they felt or feel about the matter.

Work place dispute
You: *Lucia, when you found out that your child had been sick and that you had not been given the message, how did you feel?*
Lucia: *I was angry, of course. He wouldn't like it if his child was sick and he didn't find out until late in the afternoon. I was mad. Then when I lost my baby sitter because of him, that really did it. He has a wife at home who takes care of his children. I'm a single parent and I don't have that luxury.*

Good baby sitters are hard to find. I don't know what I'm going to do.

You: *What other feelings do you have about the situation?*

Lucia: *Obviously, there's a problem here. Hernandez doesn't think I'm pulling my weight, and that bothers me. But I do my best under the circumstances.*

You: *Any other feelings either at the time or now?*

Lucia: *Well, I just want to see this get resolved and be able to move on. I can't work like this.*

You: *Hernandez, you obviously have strong feelings about the number of phone calls that Lucia receives. How have you felt about all of this?*

Hernandez: *I feel the situation is very unfair. She spends all of her time on the phone while I do all the work. I know I'm exaggerating a little, but I just feel like I am being taken advantage of. It's not fair. And about the messages, she just gets so many phone calls. I'm tired of taking messages and then listening to her on the phone in the next office chitchatting away with her friends. I'm sorry that I didn't give her this message. I now know it was important. I should have given it to her, and now I'm sorry I didn't. And, yes, I'm sure it is difficult to get a good baby sitter. I am sorry this whole thing happened, but I guess things were just coming to a head and this may be best in the long run.*

You: *Other feelings? Then or now?*

Hernandez: *I guess not. I would just like to see us resolve this as well. This is a good job. It wouldn't be easy to find another one like it. I think we can work together, but I do think we need to have a new understanding about these things.*

If you noticed, I suggested that you ask each participant pointedly, *how do you feel now?* This tends to facilitate apologies and to solidify any positive gains made up to that point.

I don't suggest you overtly ask for apologies. To me, a forced apology is worse than no apology at all. If I were a disputant, I'd prefer that any apology from my adversary come unsolicited and voluntarily. If, however, one of the parties seeks an apology as part of an acceptable resolution, deal with that as an issue in the *Agreement* stage.

Neighborhood dispute

You: *Helen, when you hurt your back raking leaves how did you feel?*

Helen: *I was angry. I know back problems are hard to fix and that there stood a good chance that I'd be in pain for quite some time. The more I thought about it the more I realized that if Frank hadn't mysteriously stopped raking them for me, then I'd never have injured myself. So it became his fault. Since the leaves came from his tree, I decided he should be responsible for them and for the consequences of not tending to them as he had in the past.*

You: *What other feelings did you have about the situation?*

Helen: *That there was no way he was going to taste another one of my pies. Since he wasn't taking care of his leaves anymore, I felt like he was taking my kindness for granted . . . even expecting* my pies.

You: *Any other feelings? Then or now?*

Helen: *I guess I was taking his help for granted, too, now that I think about it.*

You: *Anything else?*

Helen: *I hate to think of having to find another mechanic as reliable as Frank. I'd just like to get things back to normal.*

You: *Frank, you obviously have strong feelings about how all this has unfolded. How did you feel when Helen approached you about her chiropractor's bills?*

Frank: *I couldn't believe that she thought I was responsible. It seemed like a pretty good stretch of the imagination, but I had no doubt that she really believed it. But if I couldn't afford to fix my riding mower I certainly couldn't afford to fix her back. It was a ludicrous request, and I thought she'd lost touch with reality.*
You: *Any other feelings? Then or now?*
Frank: *I probably should have told her that it's not that I didn't want to pick up her leaves anymore, but that I couldn't. But I thought that was obvious. I'll cut the tree down if it will solve the problem, but I'd rather not.*
You: *Anything else?*
Frank: *I did feel she was taking me for granted. Now, I'd just like to get all this behind us and go on being good neighbors. I haven't had a decent apple pie in a long time.*

Resolution

Step 9: The agreement

Unless you feel that there are some loose ends that need to be tied in either the *Getting the facts, Question and response* or *Exploring feelings* stages, you may continue to the next phase: *Agreement.*

It takes about an hour or so to reach this point depending on the nature of the dispute. After an hour, gauge the comfort level of your participants, their energy level and the momentum of the session. If you are reasonably confident that your participants have met with a certain degree of understanding and reconciliation and that an agreement is imminent, move on. When you are writing up the agreement, it is a good time for the participants to take a break if they wish. Of course, if they are in need of performing certain bodily functions or require a cigarette during the session, it would be prudent to honor such requests and allow for a recess.

Facilitate the agreement by soliciting resolutions. Most people are self-interested, doing things that are in their interest. This is not necessarily bad. As an advocate of the mediation process, use this tendency to your advantage while attempting to gain their participation in the outcome. It is always best to allow resolutions to spring from the participants including concepts of what the alternatives to a resolution might be. Begin the *Agreement* phase of the session in the same speaking order that you have all along.

Work place dispute
You: *What are each of you willing to do, or refrain from doing, that would help us settle this matter? Lucia?*
Lucia: *Obviously, I want to receive all my phone messages, especially important ones.*
You: *Hernandez, is this agreeable?*
Hernandez: *Yeah, sure.*
You: *Lucia, may I assume that you are willing to do the same?*
Lucia: *Certainly.*
You: *Hernandez, what is it you'd like to see happen or not happen?*
Hernandez: *If I agree to pass along all of her phone messages, I'd like her to limit her personal calls to only what's essential.*
You: *Lucia?*
Lucia: *Well, I am certainly willing to limit the number of my phone calls, but what does he mean by 'essential'?*
Hernandez: *Only those calls that are very important, not just your kids calling to chitchat, or your mother calling about going shopping.*
Lucia: *I can't control who calls me.*
Hernandez: *Can you ask those people who call you frequently not to call unless they can't wait to call you in the evening at home?*

RESOLVING CONFLICT ONCE AND FOR ALL

Lucia: *I guess I could do that. If you realize that on occasion I might get a call that you might not categorize as 'essential' just because I can't control every person who calls me.*

Hernandez: *I realize that and I'm willing to be flexible as long as the calls are significantly reduced and you are able to hold up your end of the work load.*

You: *What I am hearing you say is that you are both willing to agree to pass on phone messages to each other and to limit your incoming phone calls as much as possible by asking those who are likely to call you to refrain from doing so unless absolutely necessary. Is that correct?*

Both nod in agreement.

Notice that we made sure each disputant would treat the other person with the same courtesy that they were insisting to be given. It's important to make sure that both disputants nod or verbalize an agreement to your summary. Now you go around one more time to make sure there are no lingering concerns.

You: *I think it's back to you, Lucia. Anything else you'd like to see happen or not happen?*

Lucia: *It has always been my assumption that we share our work equally. I don't want to see us change our expectations about our work schedules. I would just like to see us resume our understanding that we are to share the work equally, and see if what we have done today helps clear up some of the problems.*

You: *What do you think about that, Hernandez?*

Hernandez: *I am willing to give it a shot. I certainly want this to work. As I said before, this is a good job when we work together. If she is willing to reaffirm that we are to share our work load equally, I will go along with that.*

You: Great. One final thought, though. I think it might be a good idea to schedule a follow up meeting for the near future to see how things have worked out. Perhaps three weeks from today. Would that be all right?

Hernandez: Fine.

Lucia: Three weeks will be enough time to see how it's working. We could call for a meeting sooner if we felt like we needed to, couldn't we?

You: Absolutely. Now, Lucia, are there any other issues that we haven't covered that you would like to discuss?

Lucia: Nope. We've covered everything on the flip chart.

You: Hernandez?

Hernandez: It's a wrap.

Neighborhood dispute

You: What would each of you like to see happen or not happen as a way to resolve this matter and to keep something like this from happening again? Helen?

Helen: I'd like the leaves to be taken care of. I have doctor's orders not to aggravate my back.

You: Frank, how do you suggest Helen takes care of her leaves?

Frank: It's really not my problem; I suggest she hire some kid. I mean, I'd agree to do it for her if my mower was running just to keep the peace. But I can't unless she's willing to split the cost of repair, and that's going to be about sixty bucks outta her pocket in advance.

You: Helen, what do you think? Would it be worth it to you to help Frank pay to get his mower working so he can pick up the leaves? Or would you rather hire someone to do it, or do you have another suggestion?

Helen: I suppose it's a lot cheaper than all the hiring I'd have to do over the years. And it's a lot cheaper than the chiropractor's adjustments I'll need if I tried to rake them myself. I'll agree as long as it's just this one time. I can't be helping him fix his mower every time it breaks down. I have to set a limit.

You: Frank, is that acceptable? Helen will split the cost of fixing your mower this time and this time only if you agree to pick up her leaves every fall from now on?

Frank: You mean forever? That's a long time.

You: Helen, would you settle for a limitation to how long Frank should be obligated to help you with your leaves in exchange for helping him fix the mower this time?

Helen: I guess he's right. The money I'm spending on his mower would probably pay for three seasons if I hired someone to rake them for me. I can limit his obligation to that."

You: Frank, is that acceptable? In exchange for Helen's financial assistance in fixing your mower, do you agree to help her with her leaves for three seasons?

Frank: That's if it lasts for three seasons. There's no promise that it will stay fixed for that long. What if something else goes out on it? Then we'll be right back where we started. Why don't I just chop the tree down and be done with it?

Helen: I'd hate to see it come to that. I'll agree to three seasons, and I'll just take the chance that your mower won't break down before then. If it does, I'll just have to accept it as the end of our contract.

Frank: Well, I'd do everything I can to fix it unless it's too expensive again, but if it is and I can't use it anymore to pick up your leaves, I don't want you asking me for a refund.

Helen: I won't. But could I count on you to help me rake should your mower not be fixable just to finish out our contract?

Frank: I suppose.

You: Let me summarize what you've agreed to so far. Helen, you are going to pay half of what it costs for Frank to fix his mower in exchange for Frank's agreement to pick up your leaves for

> the next three seasons. Frank, if your mower goes bad again and it's too expensive to fix, you agree to help Helen rake her leaves until the three years are up. Helen, if his mower goes bad again, you won't seek a refund as long as he helps you rake until the three years have passed. Is this correct?

Both nod.

You: Frank, what else, if anything, would you like to see happen or not happen as a result of this session?

Frank: I'd like her to get real about my paying for her chiropractor.

You: Helen, can you release Frank from responsibility for your chiropractor's bills.

Helen: I suppose. If he keeps his part of the deal I won't be aggravating my back and needing adjustments.

You: It's to you, Helen. Is there anything else you would you like to see happen or not happen.

Helen: I'd like a copy of the receipt so that I can be sure that I paid half instead of all of the bill. And I'd like Frank to make himself available as my mechanic again.

You: Frank, would either of those requests be a problem?

Frank: No.

You: Okay, Frank. Is there anything else you'd like to see happen or not happen?

Frank: I don't mind letting you use my apples for your church bake sale as long as I can still get a couple freebies.

You: Helen, any problem baking two extra pies for Frank each year of the agreement?

Helen: Of course not.

You: Great. I think we need to set a timetable for compliance here, though. Frank, how long will it take to fix the mower once Helen pays her half in advance?

Frank: *Couple days. I can do the labor; it's the part that's too expensive for me to swing by myself. I can fix it and have both our yards done by Sunday night.*
You: *Is that acceptable, Helen?*
Helen: *That would be really nice.*
You: *Let me summarize again. In addition to the agreement on how to handle Helen's leaves, Helen agrees not to hold Frank responsible for her chiropractor bills. Helen also agrees to provide Frank with two pies each year made from the apples of his tree. Frank, you agree to provide Helen with a copy of the receipt for the part she is helping you purchase to fix your mower; you also agree to have her leaves picked up by Sunday evening; and you agree to make yourself available as Helen's mechanic again. Are these agreements correct?*
Both nod.
You: *Fantastic. One final thought, though. Do you think it might be a good idea to schedule a follow up meeting for the near future to see how things have worked out?*
Frank: *Yeah, fine.*
Helen: *You know, I'm comfortable with our agreement and pretty sure everything is going to work out. Why don't we just call you if we have any problems and we can schedule another meeting?*
You: *By all means. Is that okay with you, Frank?*
Frank: *Sure.*
You: *Are there any other issues that you would like discussed?*
Frank: *No, that's pretty much it.*
You: *Helen?*
Helen: *Nope. Everything on your flip chart has been taken care of.*

Step 10: Addressing future conflicts

At this point, even though everyone seems content, it's time to be realistic. Just because you've mediated this dispute, it doesn't mean that this fire won't rekindle over some other issue. What you want to do is to empower the disputants with the tools to prevent future disputes from getting similarly out of hand. Taking an extra step here will help prevent them from needing mediation again. Using the same techniques you've used to bring them together, they can negotiate directly to resolve future disputes with each other or with other adversaries. Solicit their willingness to solve future conflicts with civility.

Work place dispute
You: *We are going to meet again in three weeks to see how things are progressing. In the meanwhile, other issues may come up that might lead to another conflict or reignite this one. Even though we are all working together, we are all human. How do you want to handle those issues if and when they occur?*

Lucia: *I think if we just try harder to communicate our feelings instead of getting huffy about things, we'll eliminate a lot of friction.*

Hernandez: *Agreed.*

You: *In the future, please feel free to come to me if you are unable to resolve problems. As your supervisor, I care about how things work between you and I want to see you be as efficient as you can be in your work. I encourage you to try the steps that we have just used in this session if or when problems arise. Everything we used today to resolve your dispute can be used to directly negotiate any dispute without a mediator. Most people just aren't equipped to solve these kinds of problems. Now you both are, don't you think?*

Both nod in approval.

Neighborhood dispute
You: *Let me ask you this: although everything seems resolved now, other issues may come up that might lead to disagree*

ment. We are all human and we are all working together. Other events might happen. How do you want to handle those issues if and when they occur?

Helen: *If something comes up and he's unable to help me with the leaves, I'd appreciate knowing why so that I don't have to think I did something wrong.*

You: *Frank, what do you think?*

Frank: *I'll try to communicate more if she will.*

You: *So you will first try to work out any future problems directly. If you are unable to resolve problems, I want you to feel free to come to me. I enjoy our neighborhood as much as you do, and I want us to continue to live in harmony. I encourage you to try the steps of mediation that we have just used and learn from the process. Everything we used today to resolve your dispute can be used in direct negotiation between two disagreeing parties without a mediator. Okay?*

Both participants agree.

Step 11: Drafting the resolution

Before the participants leave, prepare the resolution in writing. They may choose to step outside the room or office while you prepare this, but it's not necessary. There will be a sense of relief that makes this step a comfortable pause for them to relax as they choose.

In drafting the settlement for the resolution, there are several factors to consider to keep it understandable and without loose ends:

- *Use simple, understandable language;*
- *If money is involved in the settlement, set a date by which the funds should be paid and who will receive payment, i.e., directly to the recipient, to an intermediary, etc.;*

CONDUCTING THE MEDIATION SESSION

- *Keep it accountable by requiring payment to be made by a personal check, cashier's check or money order;*
- *Identify the parties by name and use the pronoun "we" as it pertains;*
- *List all conditions separately;*
- *Make no mention of fault, blame, or guilt.*

At the end of the agreement, include a statement to this effect: *If further problems arise that we cannot resolve ourselves, we can request mediation from this or another trained mediator.*

If the situation is a matter that could lead to court action or does involve court action, it is important that you give the participants the option to consult with separate attorneys before signing any agreement. Also, if court action is possible, I would recommend that you ask them if they are willing to agree that, as long as the agreement is fulfilled, they will refrain from seeking further criminal or civil action over any event that has occurred prior to the mediation date. Otherwise, you are now ready to apply the final polish.

Work place dispute

You: *Now that you have viewed the proposed agreement, make sure that this what you intended for it to say. If you have any hesitation about signing this agreement, feel free to take it to a confidant or advisor. Remember, you don't have to sign this at this point. But if you choose to do so, it will go into both of your personnel files and will be the only record of this meeting. However, you should not fear any retribution for having this on file because the company states in its policy on disputes that mediation is to be encouraged and participants are not to be penalized in any way for having participated in a mediation session.*

Allow your participants to react and respond accordingly. After the signing, you should thank both of them for being willing to use mediation as a way to resolve their dispute. Feel free to offer carefully worded, positive observations of the session, and invite them to share theirs. Encourage handshakes as a solidifying gesture by shaking hands with each participant. Just as you didn't ask either to apologize during the *Exploring feelings* phase, don't ask them to shake hands with each other either. Rather, allow them to do so on their own accord. There is, however, nothing wrong with facilitating a pregnant pause. Escort your participants out of the room.

Neighborhood dispute
You: You have seen the agreement. Make sure it is what you intend for it to say before you sign. If you are at all unsure about the terms of the agreement and how they will affect you, feel free to take it to an advisor or confidant. There is no pressure for you to sign it at this point. When it is signed, it will become the only record of this session.

As you can see in the above scenarios, you as mediator remained neutral during the entire process and neither did nor said anything that could be construed to be biased. Protecting the integrity of the mediation process is essential in mediating all disputes. These elements are of utmost concern to participants and, therefore, should be guarded for the sake of your credibility and the credibility of mediation as a viable alternative in dispute resolution. We will discuss these and other qualities of a successful mediator in the next chapter.

Summarizing the steps
To summarize, the steps of a mediation session are a well-established unbroken sequence designed to generate a dialogue toward resolution and healing.

CONDUCTING THE MEDIATION SESSION

Opening Remarks
    Step 1: The welcome and introduction
    Step 2: Explain the voluntary nature of mediation
    Step 3: Explain your role as mediator
    Step 4: Agreement on the ground rules
    Step 5: Review the agenda

Exploring Facts and Feelings
    Step 6: Getting the facts
    Step 7: Question and response
    Step 8: Exploring feelings

Resolution
    Step 9: The agreement
    Step 10: Addressing future conflicts
    Step 11: Drafting the resolution

When strictly adhered to, this format can be applied successfully to a wide variety of disputes. Now that you know the basics, let's fine tune the process and introduce some techniques and considerations that can help crystallize a resolution. To my knowledge, the secrets I'm about to disclose have not been offered in any other mediation book and collectively have the power to induce a resolution in some cases when one would otherwise not occur.

Section 3:
The Dynamics of Mediation

A long dispute means that both parties are wrong.
—Voltaire

Creating a Favorable Mediation Environment

When making preparations for the mediation setting, there is a maxim to remember: Everything Matters. Your style of mediation matters; the furniture matters; its arrangement matters; the colors of the room matter; the lighting matters; even how you sit matters. Everything matters. Remember, *mediators sweat the details*. This doesn't mean you have to research behavioral journals to see which color tie you should wear to the session or if you should even wear one at all, but your disputants need to feel comfortable and safe. Your impact on the mediation environment can facilitate a resolution immeasurably.

Mediation models

There exists three basic models of mediation: the *automatic caucus*, the *problem-solving*, and the *expressive* models. All professional mediators use a variation of these depending on the nature of the conflicts they mediate and their own personal preference.

In the automatic caucus model, the attorneys of the disputants give their opening statements in each other's presence, and then the mediator immediately exiles each party to separate quarters. The mediator then shuttles between them attempting to hammer out an agreement. The two parties reunite to sign the document when and if they reach a resolution. Although these are sometimes rapid sessions, the mediator has more control over the outcome than the disputants, which may account for the fact that this is less successful than the other models with only a 50 to 75 percent success rate. In the problem-solving model, disputants tell their version of the story and then collectively brainstorm a resolution under the supervision of the mediator. These are very efficient approaches designed to move a conflict to resolution quickly. Neither process, however, builds in an opportunity for the disputants to express how the conflict has affected them personally or to vent their feelings—a step that invites conciliation and healing.

The model I use, teach and have detailed in this book I call the expressive model. It borrows from victim-offender mediation (an application of mediation I discuss in Section 4 under *Other Applications*) in that it allows offenders and their victims to express their feelings en route to facilitating a resolution. I further modify this process for disputes by adding a phase that invites disputants to ask questions and respond to what the other side has said or asked. By allowing for a thorough airing of issues, feelings and options for resolution, this model empowers the participants rather than the mediator and places as much emphasis on the process as it does the resolution. Nothing contributes more to creating a favorable mediation environment. I use this model exclusively and find it to be successful 75 to 95 percent of the time.

Location

The location of the mediation setting should be perceived by both parties as *neutral* and *private*. For the sake of assuring neutrality, neither side should have the home court advantage. Lucia and Hernandez aren't going to feel comfortable meeting in the other's house or office. The imbalance of power by meeting on either of the disputant's turf is enough to sink a battleship. Likewise, Helen won't feel comfortable in Frank's workshop any more than Frank would feel at ease in Helen's kitchen. There are too many tools (read: weapons) around, the exact location of which are known to only one of the disputants. A neutral, off-site location agreeable to both parties may be best but only if the site also guarantees the second most important aspect of location: *privacy.*

When privacy is threatened, confidentiality—one of mediation's prime features—is threatened as well. Your efforts to preserve this will guarantee the parties that they won't be interrupted, distracted or rattled by passersby. Also, they know they won't be seen coming or going to the session—a factor that may be more important to them than you might think. *The more sensitive the dispute, the harder you should strive for a private setting.*

Lighting

Harsh spotlights make people feel as if they are being interrogated. Dim lights can make people feel vulnerable and threatened. Florescent lights can feel cold and harsh. Try to provide warm, moderate lighting if possible. You want your participants to feel comfortable and your lighting should invite cooperation, or at least not inhibit it.

Color

This will be difficult to control, but when choosing your site keep this in mind: *avoid red*. Red has long been associated with anger, violence, animosity and temper. Teachers and child psychologists know that red is an inflammatory color that shortens attention spans and creates a sense of urgency. In her book *The Language of Color* (Warner Books, 1988), Dorothee Mella says that reds work to provoke emotions, increase energy, and create highly charged environments; greens impart feelings of practicality, tranquility, and healing; light blues calm emotions and are supportive; dark blues are cold and businesslike; yellows promote feelings of sharing and facilitate communication; and browns are stabilizing colors that add warmth and feelings of security. You might not have access to rooms with color schemes that are the most conducive to mediation, but it is in the best interest of your objective to avoid antagonizing hues.

The great table debate

The subject of whether or not to use a table within the arrangement is subject to personal preference. Professional mediators argue opposing philosophies. From a physical standpoint, a table could be considered a barrier between the members of the session. In the case of a tempestuous participant determined to sabotage the session, a table could interfere with an act of physical aggression. For mediators who are uncomfortable with a high level of conflict, a table offers a comforting barrier of security.

Tables mean business, especially square ones. Some disputants may view a table as an icon of intended progress and would welcome the serious intent to reach a solution that a table suggests; others would consider it something to pound a fist upon during hard negotiations and would become immediately defensive before the session even began. The prospect of such theatrics is intimidating.

It's difficult to guess what frame of mind a table would put your disputants in, but you can bet it will influence their perception of the mediation process as either inviting or antagonistic. The worst case scenario is that both disputants would be intimidated. So why not employ the cooperative influence that a circular table would promote? Say, a round coffee table. The design is certainly more comfortable and homey, invites a unity of purpose, is less business-like and is too low for fist pounding.

Many mediators embrace this table/no table compromise, and I am not entirely opposed to it. After one particularly provocative mediation session, however, I was grateful that a table did not exist. The case involved a disputant who claimed that his neighbor had been shooting his geese. The neighbor denied the offense. Suddenly, the claimant ask to be excused momentarily. Moments later, he returned to the room carrying a large burlap bag that he immediately upended allowing the contents to tumble onto the floor between us. A dead goose lay at our feet. Seizing upon our stunned silence, he offered the goose as evidence of his neighbor's guilt. In my eyes the man proved three things: first, he was the owner of a dead goose; secondly, he watches too much television; and thirdly, if I had used a table for the session, it would have likely been marred. I've not used one since.

Personally, I think tables are unnecessary and interfere with the process. I don't care if it's square, round, heart-shaped or a stump in the woods, a table is a barrier, and the job of a mediator is to remove barriers. Also, when there's furniture between me and the disputants it keeps me from reading their body language, a telling indicator of their disposition and mood swings. With a table between you and the participants, suffice it to say that much is lost.

Body language

Volumes have been written regarding body language, and it is beyond the scope of this book to address all of them with their many interpretations. As an occasional mediator you won't be as attuned to interpreting body language as a professional mediator, but two attitudes, willingness and stubbornness, send non-verbal signals long before they become blatant verbal statements. An accurate assessment as to their intensity provides an advance warning so that you can head off an impasse.

Look for avoidance behavior to tip you off to an impending objection. Limited or no eye contact between the participants and between the participants and you, a closed body posture (arms folded, legs crossed) and rigid shoulders are defensive postures that signal inflexibility.

Be on the watch for indicators of aggression and anxiety as well: eyebrows drawn inward (tension), sitting on the edge of one's seat (doesn't intend on staying long, or is prepared to pounce), nervous idiosyncrasies (nail biting, knee bouncing, general fidgeting, etc.). Don't expect a physical confrontation, but be ready for anything. While you are attuned to other's signals, be ever mindful of what your own nuances communicate to the disputants. Your posture and body language should communicate interest and involvement. Just as folding your arms across your chest indicates inflexibility and close mindedness, leaning back in your chair with your hands interlaced behind your head indicates indifference. It also makes it difficult to catch a dead goose. A comfortable mix between formality and informality reflects a proper balance between your roles as facilitator and participant.

Seating Orientation

The session won't be a marathon, so furniture is not crucial. The chairs should be comfortable. Simply avoid the extremes: no granite slabs and no bean bag chairs. More important than the type of chairs is how you and the participants are arranged. Avoid seating your antagonists opposite each other. At first, they won't feel comfortable looking each other straight in the eye, so I wouldn't force such an encounter. Such settings are considered confrontational and in mediation, confrontations are counter-productive.

By the same token, sitting the disputants side-by-side, both facing the mediator, places too much emphasis on the mediator's role in the session. It also makes it difficult for the disputants to speak to each other. They would have to turn their heads and/or bodies to speak to each other, an awkward and forced gesture that creates tension.

The seating orientation for a mediation session is an excellent opportunity to put symbolism into practice. Think circles. Circles—a symbol of peace, unity and love—have permeated events and rituals in many cultures for generations. Wedding bands, the intersecting Olympic rings, halos, even the way we encircle with our arms those whom we embrace are all symbols of unity.

No culture believes in the healing power of circles more than the aborigines of Canada. They have used circles in their culture for healing, sharing and sentencing those who commit crimes against their society for generations. "Healing circles" enable their people to overcome the victimizations that accompany alcoholism and domestic abuse. Not a punishment-oriented culture, these native Canadians believe that circular arrangements empower individuals to bring offenders back into the fold and, therefore, harmony back to their communities by linking the personal energy fields that many feel surround every individual.

"Sharing circles" are perhaps the most common exploitation of circles in this aboriginal culture. Members sit in circular formation—concentric circles in the case of numerous participants—and pass a stone or stick from person to person. The object is held as each member of the group shares thoughts, triumphs or tragedies until the object has made its way around each circle.

Justice in this aboriginal culture is served in the context of a "sentencing circle." Again using a circular arrangement, the court convenes and the judge hands down a sentence. The circle brings an element of unity to the proceedings and invites healing.

Since mediation attempts to repair a break in unity, arranging your disputants in a circular setting facilitates cooperation and reconciliation. This means not having empty chairs within the circular arrangement, which serve as breaks in the circular flow of energy. But what if there are only three participants in a mediation session—two disputants and you, the mediator? Regardless of the number, each participant should be able to view the other equally. An equilateral triangle approximates the same symbolism as a circle. The Egyptians built pyramids using this shape. They believed, and many others still do today, that the geometric nature of the pyramid holds immeasurable power. So don't worry too much if your participants view the arrangement as a circle or triangle. In either case, if you angle the chairs toward the center of the arrangement you will be getting the maximum psychological benefit out of the orientation.

Keep the disputants about three feet apart so as to discourage physical contact in the event the situation gets out of hand. In mediation, however, this is rarely the case since those who agree to a mediation session do so with the intention of resolving their dispute. Well, almost everybody. A minister once came after me physically for trying to squelch his verbal abuse of his adversary, his mother. Needless to say, getting them to resolve their dispute through mediation would have taken longer than walking blindfolded to Pluto. But other than that, I've never experienced hostility in a mediated setting that led to physical aggression.

This is probably because participants see the mediator as a peacemaker. Rarely will people who agree to mediate embark on something as damaging to the process as physical violence. As long as you, the mediator, feel confident in your role and capable of handling any situation that arises, a circular or triangular seating arrangement with no table is preferable with the disputants at least three feet apart.

If a co-mediator participates in the session, I suggest that he or she sit directly opposite the lead mediator. This facilitates good eye contact and allows the mediators to experience the session from opposite viewpoints. Positioning both mediators together presents an *us-against-them* orientation and could facilitate antagonism.

The qualities of a successful mediator
- **Good mediators are good listeners.** They maintain eye contact, don't interrupt and concentrate on the verbal and nonverbal messages others send them. They don't fidget and they aren't

so busy constructing their response while someone is still speaking that they aren't listening effectively. They often ask speakers to clarify or restate their message.
- **Good mediators are good communicators.** They ask questions to make sure the messages they have received are accurate. They choose their words carefully and speak directly to the object of their expressions. They are in control of their emotions and don't respond destructively or in angry outbursts. They respond directly to questions asked of them and express their thoughts exactly as they are, always choosing neutral words over inflammatory terms.
- **Good mediators are compassionate.** They want to relieve the tension that exists between people and groups. They strive to extinguish animosity, stress, pain, aggression and destructive behaviors for the greater good of individuals and groups. They look for ways to help those in distress and find great comfort in having brought peace to situations and peace of mind to family, friends, acquaintances, and strangers.
- **Good mediators are facilitators.** It is not a mediator's place to resolve the conflict. Remember that the disputants came to the session because they want a resolution but don't know how to bring it about. For you to help them do that you must secure their trust. It means being honest, open and unflappable when tempers flare. It means maintaining the process no matter what. Previsualizing an outcome helps. We'll discuss that in Section 3 under *Advanced Mediation*.
- **Good mediators remain neutral**. First and foremost, you must assure your disputants that you are not biased in the case. Even though an element of partiality may occasionally be lurking within, your job is to assure your participants that you have separated yourself from your biases. When you project neutrality, you build their trust. You should also avoid mediating cases in which you have a conflict of interest or have a signif-

icant relationship with one of the parties. Your only interest should be in the resolution of the conflict. Also, you may not qualify to mediate a dispute in which you have a vested interest in a particular outcome.

- **Good mediators respect confidentiality.** You can be as neutral as a fencepost, but if you go telling everybody else in town what was said over the rail, you'll soon be firewood. Nobody is going to trust you with their feelings if they don't have the confidence that their thoughts, insecurities, misgivings, or predicaments will go no further. Establish your confidentiality early and your disputants will be ready to trust you.

- **Good mediators establish structure.** An offer to put your participants through an established process designed for the resolution of their dispute creates confidence in your ability to move them beyond their conflict. When they know you have a proven tool to bring their conflict to a conclusion—especially when that tool appears to be more hospitable than litigation—trusting your willingness to use that tool can seem to be the path of least resistance.

- **Good mediators exude confidence.** If you project the belief that your disputants have the ability to resolve their differences, they will be more apt to believe it themselves. Disputants who know that you have faith in their abilities even when they have no faith in themselves are willing to trust that you might know their potential better than they do. To those embroiled in disputes, that's comforting to know, and they are more likely to trust you with the process.

Once you have secured the trust of the participants by fulfilling these obligations, you have several other responsibilities as a mediator. These are more active responsibilities that may require you to react to obstacles that may arise throughout the mediation process. They include:

Focusing

Mediators keep the dialogue from deteriorating into a melee by keeping a sharp focus on the process. This is achieved by not allowing the exchanges to drift too far away from the channels that a successful session should follow.

Probing

If there appear to be underlying issues upon which the conflict arose, good mediators probe beneath the surface to reveal them. Exposing these roots and addressing them is essential to many resolutions.

Exploring

Good mediators are tour guides. They lead their participants through the deep recesses of the conflict. They allow their participants to examine their own feelings, motives and objectives and invite them to search through a myriad of solutions while illuminating the alternatives to mediation. If no solution seems worth pursuing to them, mediators invite them to create their own.

Perspective

The first casualty of a dispute is perspective. Loss of perspective is so much at the heart of deadlocked disputes that I've dedicated an entire heading to it in Section 3 under *Advanced Mediation*. For now, suffice it to say that infusing perspective back into a conflict is one of the greatest commodities a mediator can provide.

It is important for you to remember that as a mediator, you are not a problem solver but a facilitator. By injecting the skills and attributes defined above into the mediation process you create an environment that encourages disputants to resolve their own conflict and pursue the healing of their relationship.

Surviving Deadlocks, Tension and Allies

When Mediation Fails

Not all scenarios are going to be as easy to resolve as Hernandez and Lucia's or Frank and Helen's. These, though typical, were simple conflicts solved by disputants without a lot of emotional baggage or hidden agendas. Nobody tried to get physical; nobody refused to cooperate; nobody was bent on sabotaging the process; nobody brought a weapon; and nobody dumped a dead goose on the floor. You may not be so lucky.

When you find yourself in the middle of a session that seems to be going nowhere at an alarming rate, don't despair. You may be deep into the woods, but you aren't without one last path toward success: *a caucus*. Caucuses are designed to break deadlocks when nothing else works. When you caucus, you break down into private sessions with each participant and try to hammer out an acceptable agreement by shuttling from one to the other. But there is danger in using this technique too soon. Before I discuss when and how to caucus, let me first discuss why you shouldn't until you are positive there is no other way to get past a deadlock.

No matter how well you preserve your sense of neutrality during the mediation session, it is inevitable that when you caucus with the parties, some trust is lost. They will wonder what is being said when you are meeting with their adversary. To some, it will reek of treachery and double-dealing. You can't help that. The atmosphere that sends mediation into caucus is, ironically, the worst time for a caucus to take place. The parties are continuing to disagree, and the tone has already turned negative. The reason you caucus is that you have nothing left to lose.

Inexperienced mediators use a caucus as an escape when emotions reach high levels; they forget that an emotional venting of frustrations can help the mediation process. The thickening of emotions is not the time for the mediator to run for the cover of a caucus. Rather, let emotions run their course as long as the parties respect the ground rules, then get on with mediation. Jumping into a caucus just to squelch the participants' angst is counterproductive. As defined in the heading *Creating a favorable mediation environment*, some mediation styles call for a caucus immediately after opening statements or the statements of the facts. I have even heard of one style of mediation in which the parties never actually meet face-to-face. They simply meet in adjacent offices while the mediator ping-pongs from room to room. I call this "he said-she said" diplomacy and don't consider it a legitimate form of mediation. Mediation is an interpersonal process. There is no way that participants can reach their own agreement if they never meet. If you as a mediator allow the caucus to replace direct negotiations, you will inhibit the participants' ability to reach their own resolution, and you will prevent their feeling a sense of ownership in the agreement.

The early or overuse of the caucus strengthens the ability of the mediator to control and manipulate the mediation process. Indeed, it may take longer for a caucus-dominated process to work because the parties do not gain the direct information they need with which to make a decision. What they get is second-hand information or even misinformation. The airing of all facts, suppositions and emotions during the steps of the mediation process is crucial. That very airing of information and feelings is what facilitates a resolution. Your decision to caucus it should only be considered if the session deadlocks in the resolution phase and should be based on certain criteria:

- *The parties are deadlocked and no solutions appear imminent or even possible;*
- *The parties continue to be so hostile that direct negotiation through you seems fruitless and counterproductive;*
- *You feel you are not getting accurate information;*
- *You need to probe the facts in a way that does not threaten anyone's confidentiality;*
- *You feel that the balance of power between the participants is so skewed that you question whether those with less power can adequately represent themselves in direct negotiation without fear.*

A caucus gives you and the participants some breathing room, time to think, and a chance to come up with new ideas or perspectives . . . or to go get the goose from the pickup. A caucus also . . .

. . . allows you and the participants the opportunity to probe underlying obstacles,
. . . unearths additional facts that were concealed during the session,
. . . allows you to point out possible weaknesses in a position,
. . . lets you question the participants' minimum requirements for a settlement,
. . . affords you with the chance to turn unrealistic demands into realistic expectations,
. . . lets the mediator try ideas out on the disputants in private.

Even though the caucus is a fluid process, you should first secure the agreement of the participants before pursuing the option. In fact, in your introductory remarks you may want to mention the possibility of a caucus so that the participants are not totally surprised when you spring into this new phase. Personally, I use the caucus so rarely that I often don't even mention the possibility.

If you feel the need to throw the session into caucus ask the disputants if it is as obvious to them as it is to you that the session has reached a roadblock. State that you have one more approach that could salvage a resolution. Explain to them that in a caucus you meet with each party separately to try to move the session along in order to facilitate an agreement.

After securing their approval, select which one of the participants you will meet with first. Choose the one you feel either has the most ground to give, is more likely to give ground or perhaps *should* give more ground in your opinion—an opinion you have kept to yourself throughout the process.

The caucus obviously necessitates the use of two rooms. If possible, avoid moving the participants in and out of one room since it's important to maintain privacy and security during the caucus. Once alone with your chosen participant, ask where he or she sees the situation to be at that point. This is taking a step back from the center of the controversy and letting your participant take an inventory of the situation. You should do the same from your standpoint.

Solicit alternatives to a negotiated settlement from the participant. This is where you illuminate the worst-case scenario should the session end in a deadlock. Fear, being the great motivator that it is, may generate renewed interest in solutions that had been previously viewed as unacceptable. Bring to light any unpleasant alternatives to a settlement that would involve expending time, money or lead to the loss of control over the outcome. Be careful, however, to pursue them without sounding as if you're giving ultimatums. If this stage is viewed as overt arm-twisting, you blew it. At this point, ask if there are any options that the participant can see or would consider as a way to settle the dispute. After considering them, or even if none is generated, you may test some of your own. How you present your solutions is important. They must be seen as *options* that the participant can either grasp or let pass. The more you are attached to your possible solutions the less likely you will present them as options; your participants will think of them as your solutions, not theirs.

If you unearth an option that you think may be agreeable to the other party, request permission to meet with the other participant, and then follow the same steps as with the first. You might be tempted to skip this step if you think the chances of agreement are a foregone conclusion, but it is important that you meet alone with the second participant regardless if for no other reason than to reinforce the perception of neutrality.

Caucuses, when entered at the right time and when employed as described here, have a high success rate. If you are still unable to break the deadlock despite your best efforts, you should simply reconvene the participants, reiterate their other alternatives and adjourn the session. Above all else, remember that mediation is successful between 75 and 95 percent of the time. Give it your best, but just as it is not appropriate for you to take credit for success, nor should you take blame for failure.

High Tension Disputes

Depending on the temperament of the disputants, conflicts can generate considerable tension during a mediation session. As a mediator, if you prepare for extremes, the mid-range takes care of itself. Low-tension disputes are readily resolved with the process outlined in this guide but high tension disputes require special skills.

One way to tell that the disputants are tense is when they refuse to look at each other. If a resolution is to materialize, the parties must sooner or later see eye-to-eye both figuratively and literally. Figuratively, it's up to them to connect. In the literal sense, however there is a technique I use to encourage them to look at each other. When either disputant, either speaking or listening, insists on looking at me instead of their adversary, I attempt to divert their gaze toward the other disputant by focusing my attention on their adversary. I'll occasionally glance at the disputant who is avoiding contact, and then center my gaze back on their adversary. When my center of focus is on someone else, it draws their attention likewise.

Anger, intimidation, power struggles and threats all contribute to a high level of anxiety for the other disputant and for the mediator. If you find yourself embroiled in a tempestuous case, there are several coping mechanisms you can use to insulate yourself from the tension.

First and foremost, remember that your disputants, angry though they may be, have entered into mediation *voluntarily*. Any anger or animosity they possess is directed at their adversary, the conflict itself or at themselves, not you. You are the peacemaker, and nobody will be angry at you for offering your services in that capacity. Therefore, remember that whatever tension exists is not directed at you.

Secondly, be mindful that verbal outbursts and terse exchanges during a session can be therapeutic. You are giving the disputants a forum for venting their anxiety. Keep telling yourself that this venting may be necessary before a resolution is possible. However, even in the heat of an emotional exchange, don't forget to keep the disputants mindful of the ground rules. Do not let them resort to name calling, finger pointing or verbally abusive language. Gentle reminders, though, should not interfere with the venting. Be calm and allow the exchange to take place without your sinking to the same level to which their venting plunges them. Give the disputants time to work through this venting, and they will rise to your level of calm as long as you are setting the standard. It's best to sit back, let the venting run its course, interject reminders of the rules only when necessary and allow tensions to exhaust themselves before advancing to the next phase.

In high tension disputes, it's more important to firmly adhere to the ground rules than in low tension disputes. That's because the elements that generate tension can easily derail the process if they are allowed to work outside of the boundaries that the rules are designed to maintain. Your attempt to arrest any violation of the rules at an early stage is needed to keep the session from spinning out of control.

Allowing tension to intimidate you almost certainly guarantees an unresolved dispute. Remember that the animosity you feel during a mediation session is not directed at you and that it facilitates a resolution. Grasp the understanding that anger often needs to be vented before a resolution can crystallize and, therefore, should be allowed to run its course. Urging the disputants to adhere to the ground rules will help the occasional mediator cope with the anxiety of a tension-filled session.

Witnesses

When disputants want to bring in witnesses it means one of two things: either you haven't explained the nature of mediation very well or the participant has a hidden agenda. In mediation you aren't trying to make liars out of anybody. You accept the participants' information at face value. Therefore, if the purpose of witnesses is for one disputant to verify the other disputant's testimony later should the case go to court, you're not getting through to somebody. Questioning the integrity of the information is counterproductive. Remember, mediation is not about ferreting out the truth. Although we solicit the facts from each disputant, we are not interested so much in a consensus on the facts as we are a resolution of the dispute in light of whatever opposing interpretations of the event exist. Instead, we buffer the disagreement by saying, "What is your point of view?"

If one of the disputants needs a witness to further a hidden agenda, it probably involves using the revelations that will come out in the session as fodder for pre-determined litigation. If you recall, however, one of the ground rules restricts using any information or statement generated during the mediation session for use in other hearings. If one of your participants wants you to allow a witness, you should use these arguments to dissuade. Explain that the facts as each party sees them don't necessarily have to agree, and that one of your ground rules will forbid anything brought out in the session to be used elsewhere.

Support persons

If the victim of a criminal act—for example, theft, assault, etc.—wants a support person allowed into the session, it's justified. In fact, it may be necessary to balance the power. But these are not the kinds of cases the occasional mediator would or should be mediating. If the case you are mediating has a massive imbalance of power, you might be out of your league. Save these for professional mediators.

However, in simple interpersonal disputes, some of your disputants may request your permission to bring in friends, family members or co-workers for moral support. While I respect their need for such support, it is not always in the best interest of the mediation process. The more people you have, the more variables you have to control. Sometimes these variables are good; sometimes they are inherently destructive.

Two types of support persons your disputants could request you allow into the session are *spokespersons* and *spectators*. First let's dismantle the spectator.

Spectators come in three colors: cheerleaders, bomb droppers and just plain excess baggage. **Cheerleaders** inhibit the process. They cheer their team and try to rile everyone else up. **Bomb droppers** drop bombs. In their private lives they enjoy poking cornered opossums with sticks for the sheer joy of infuriating them. They won't rest until they make the dispute worse. Spectators as **excess baggage** aren't as antagonistic as bomb droppers, but your disputants may feel pressured to perform as their audience wishes they would instead of how they really want to react.

Let's say you're involved in a post-divorce dispute over property. Considering that a divorce dispute can be pretty heavy stuff, let's say that all other issues pertaining to this particular divorce have been settled, but a dispute arises over who gets the dog. Using the techniques I've detailed, you're probably capable of keeping the case out of court. But let's suppose the ex-husband, ex-wife or both want to bring their new lovers in for support. Suddenly, you've got problems. It doesn't take a Ph.D to figure out that the tension these spectators could bring to your session is immeasurable.

Another reason to exclude all but the disputants is to maintain balance. If any of your disputants are troublemakers in the environment in which the dispute arose, everyone will be against that person. Obviously, you want to limit the opponents in the session so that the despised individual doesn't feel outnumbered. Whatever spectators intend to become, one fact remains: *if you have spectators, you have dead weight.*

Spokespersons are just as unnecessary. Speaking through a representative demonstrates a lack of sincerity and a weak commitment to a resolution. There are, however, two exceptions: cases involving group conflicts and juveniles.

In disputes that involve, or resolutions that will directly affect, a group of individuals, having a spokesperson bears consideration. Try to get large, unwieldy groups to choose a few designated spokespersons so that you can work directly with the smallest number of participants possible. Be careful, however. If you try to exclude people who have a legitimate stake in the outcome from the session, they may either try to assert themselves destructively behind the scenes or sabotage the agreement altogether.

You can weave the legitimate secondary disputants into the process later if the situation warrants their inclusion. First, exclude secondary disputants from the preliminary session, but bring them in later to announce the agreement and invite them to support the resolution. Your objective here is to let the principals forge their agreement and then see if the secondary disputants will buy into it or suggest modifications to facilitate a group-wide acceptance. The risk here is that the group will attempt to alter the resolution to such a degree that it is no longer acceptable to the principal disputants. Keeping your focus on the main players is crucial in avoiding this scenario.

There are cases, however, when numbers don't provide the balance but personality does. I mediated a case where everyone in a department ganged up against one fellow who was trying to control the whole office without the authority to do so. Everyone in the session was against this guy except me. I allowed the imbalance in numbers because he had a very strong personality and could easily overpower the other disputants in the case, a personality trait that drew him into the conflict the first place. He held his own pretty well, and on balance the two sides were equivalent.

In cases that involve juveniles, parents tend to want to speak for their children. Although they may try to dominate the discussion, if you exclude them from the process you may be trampling their rights. Therefore, don't actively discourage their presence or participation. This is an excellent opportunity to tap into the power that comes from circular arrangements. Seat the juveniles in a small center circle, then position the parents around and slightly behind them so that you have two concentric circles. Inform all those present of the ground rules and proceed. As you advance from phase to phase, volley the questions and responses between yourself and the main disputants. Then volley each phase of the session from the inner circle to the outer circle to include the secondary disputants. Proceed with the standard steps of mediation giving the main participants the first chance to speak, then opening it up to the outer circle by saying, "Okay, do any of you have facts or feelings that have not come out?" Progressing from inner circle to outer circle enhances the process and gives everyone a feeling of ownership in the outcome. This may sound tedious, but some of the steps into the outer circle can go quickly.

Placing the parent(s) behind the juvenile(s) is symbolic of their support. In your opening remarks, explain the symbolism of their placement. Although the session may be easier without them, they can contribute to the resolution if they are appropriately involved. To facilitate their positive contribution to the process, tell them you're glad they're there and that they are to serve primarily as advisors. Explain to them that in the *Getting the facts* stage they may state information that has not been revealed.

Attorneys

In the view of many mediators, the appropriate use of attorneys in mediation is in giving independent legal advice to their clients whether it be during a mediation session or outside the session before the disputants actually sign the agreement. Throughout the process impress upon your participants that *mediation is a substitute for litigation, not sound legal advice.* In all cases that are being handled by an attorney—even when attorneys are involved in the case but not present—you should give the disputants every opportunity to review the agreement with their attorneys before signing it, especially in divorce mediation. It's in their best interest and shows respect for the role the attorney plays.

Be mindful that attorneys are creatures of habit as we all are. Some, especially trial lawyers, are not accustomed to making statements in formal hearings like mediation; they bring out the facts by questioning witnesses. Out of habit, they may simply ask their clients questions to bring out facts that haven't surfaced. This is not necessarily bad except that it belabors the process. You may explain in your opening remarks that, because you are accepting everything at face value, they need not ask questions but simply state the facts as they know them.

Attorneys may not have personal "feelings" about the issue or might not feel comfortable verbalizing them in mediation. Therefore, try phrasing it differently to bring them into the proceedings. Instead of asking for "feelings," solicit their "concerns." They may express concerns about their client agreeing to this or that. As in group disputes, alternate from the inner to outer circle to maximize the main participants' contributions and minimize the involvement of their attorneys without excluding them from the process. When you have their support they can be a part of the solution instead of part of the problem.

When either party is being unrealistic about what might come out of a court hearing or the mediation session, I may send them back to their attorneys to talk over their expectations. I will suggest they have their attorney advise them on their chances of prevailing with their demands. I'll also refer them to an attorney if I feel they are getting misinformation from other sources about alternatives to mediation. When it's appropriate, I will offer information without indicating bias. A mediator's information must always be factual and may not take the form of advice.

In a few cases I have actually requested attorneys to be present. If I feel the parties are too antagonistic to be realistic about a resolution, and if I know their attorneys are supportive of a resolution, I'll invite them into the session—with the permission of the disputants, of course.

Generally, I let the disputing parties make the final decision to bring in their attorneys since they'll have to foot the expense. One case in particular showed the value of this approach. A couple who had been involved for years and had created a household were splitting up. There were intense feelings of betrayal, animosity and bitterness. An outside relationship added to the chemistry of the conflict. We had several sessions and got close to agreement, but we couldn't quite get there. I knew their attorneys were supportive of mediation, so I requested a final meeting with the attorneys present, hoping they would help me hammer out a resolution. I wanted them to say, "Hey, this is a pretty good deal. You're not going to get better than this without risking a loss." That's exactly what happened. Coming from me, though, that would have meant nothing. Nor could I say it and maintain my appearance of neutrality. The attorneys provided the advice that I did not have the authority to deliver. The outcome probably would not have been satisfactory without the attorneys' involvement.

In insurance disputes, I always advise legal representation. The balance of power is too great on the side of insurance companies for people to represent themselves without an attorney. In these cases, attorneys will be paid roughly one third of the settlement for their representation just as if the case went to trial. The difference is that in mediation, participants with attorneys still have control over the outcome.

Advanced Mediation

Perspective through visualization

One of the qualities a successful mediator brings to a dispute is an element that the participants have lost: *perspective*. People who are bitterly embroiled in a conflict look at their dispute through a microscope. They analyze every petty element in such great detail that it is impossible for them to see that the dispute is just one facet of their life that happens to be without harmony. As a result, they allow their lives to revolve around the dispute instead of letting the dispute remain as one of many elements that affect their lives. Perspective is lost and the dispute becomes bigger than life itself, overshadowing everything and permeating virtually every waking thought. They become obsessed with it as if nothing else matters. They lose sleep, productivity, time, peace of mind and their temper—often at loved ones or those not even involved in the dispute.

A mediator takes the microscope away from those who are over-analyzing their disputes, gives them a wide-angle lens, then asks, "Now what do you see?" Perspective. It means showing the disputants what's really there in relation to the big picture. It means illuminating reality. It means allowing no element to burden an individual or a situation with more than its actual net weight. A lack of perspective not only invites dispute but impedes its resolution. By maintaining perspective, mediators empower themselves with another gift: *visualization.*

Visualizing a successful resolution isn't natural, especially for new mediators. It's just too easy to become wrapped up in the process to have an eye toward the outcome. But if mediators can consider the destination while orchestrating the journey, a successful resolution is much more likely to occur. Explaining how to visualize an outcome is like explaining how to climb a tree. You just do it. The only thing you have to know is that you can.

By visualizing an outcome, I don't mean preconceiving a particular resolution as you would like to see it; that's not your place. Rather, it means visualizing that a resolution will occur and that the disputants will be leaving the session with the conflict behind them. You anticipate the cathartic effect of the feeling phase and that it will lead to remorse in one or both of the participants and, subsequently, fuel the resolution. When you visualize, you become one with the resolution. You know in your mind where the session is headed—not what you feel the specific terms of the agreement should be, but in a more general way—and you anticipate the intermediate steps that will signify progress to you. Then you set out to facilitate each step. When you visualize, the steps fall like dominos. The trick is to facilitate each step through that visualization. Here's how:

Communicate hope—One of the main tasks of the mediator is to communicate to disputants that there is hope that they can resolve their dispute. Since disputants aren't usually optimistic, it helps if you impart confidence that they will rise above their animosity. One of the more powerful things a mediator can do is to maintain a constant "Hey, you can do it" attitude. Provide that encouragement. Be their cheerleader. Show them you know that deep down inside they have the ability to construct a peaceful resolution that will put this anxiety behind them. Disputants are too mired in the negative to hope for themselves. But you have to be dogged about it because when things look hopeless and people are caught up in their antagonism its easy to say, "Look at yourselves! You're behaving like children!" It takes a lot of patience to stand back and maintain objectivity and hopefulness in light of how low human behavior can descend, but you must. In contentious disputes, being a referee and maintaining an attitude that *they-can-do-it-if-they-stick-with-it* is the only thing you can do. And it's the best thing you can do.

- **Measuring dispositions**—Visualizing depends in part on sizing up the situation so that you can assess those steps toward resolution that may cause you the most trouble. We subconsciously size up people every day. Fair or not, it's human nature to make assumptions about a person's inner character or mood at first blush. Mediators have to fine tune this impulse and work it to the advantage of the session.

    You already know the nature of the *dispute* before the session, but you may not know the nature of the *disputants.* Within the first few minutes and during your introductory remarks you have to get a feeling quickly and accurately for the temperaments that came into the room. Interpret their verbal and non-verbal clues to tell you how they communicate, how they argue, how they feel about each other, the level of conflict, the level of animosity, how they feel about being in the session, etc. Make an assessment of where they seem to be in terms of anger, anxiety, fear and nervousness so that when they change, the difference is detectable. Detectable changes indicate that a swing in their attitude is imminent. This could be good or bad, but knowing it's coming gives you the edge.
- **Verbalize success**—The first step to healing is to visualize it. Sometimes I will even verbalize a visualization just to let the disputants know that I'm looking beyond the dispute to a scenario that is entirely possible and much more pleasing than their conflict, should they be able to resolve their dispute peacefully. Because people are so mired in their conflict, someone else needs to visualize what could lie beyond for them. For example, toward the end of the meeting I might say to Frank and Helen, "There's no reason why you two can't go

back to chats at the fence in the shade of the apple tree again when the only thing on your minds is the weather." To Hernandez and Lucia I might say, "I don't see why you two couldn't blow the top off of the sales chart and collect the bonuses that go with it if you could only put this behind you."

Extracting remorse—One of the key pivot points I look for that tells me a resolution is imminent is for one or both parties to express remorse. That's the final tumbler of the lock that frees the disputants from the shackles of the conflict. But remorse isn't easy for people to admit. Unfortunately, some interpret remorse as a sign of weakness. Mediators see it as a sign of character and integrity. When you sense that there are feelings of remorse lingering just beneath the surface but neither has the courage to let them out, there are ways to facilitate the process. The question "How do you feel now?" usually brings it out if it is to come out at all. I ask it during the feeling phase of the process right after I've asked the disputants how they felt at the time of the incident.

When it works, it works with great effect. Occasionally it works with great effect and a few chuckles. I once mediated a dispute between an apartment tenant and a cable television company. The cable company claimed the tenant had pirated its cable services by manipulating the external cable wiring outside his apartment and filed charges of criminal mischief and theft against the tenant. During the session, the tenant admitted that he did indeed hook a cable wire to his television, but denied damaging the external box to make it work. He was an easy-going country boy who remained refreshingly candid throughout the session. His blunt honesty relaxed us all. In the feeling phase I asked how he felt at the time he realized he had rigged free cable services for himself.

THE DYNAMICS OF MEDIATION

"Surprised! I didn't think it would be that easy to get cable!"

"Then how did you feel?" I asked.

"I was happy! Then I got bored. There were too many ball games . . . and I didn't get the Disney Channel." I pressed for remorse.

"Then how did you feel?"

"Then I was happy again." he said.

"Why?"

"Happy that I wasn't paying for such boring programs!"

As comical as his honesty was, he had not one iota of remorse for pirating what he termed to be "boring programming." Nevertheless, because of his candor the dispute was resolved successfully and remains one of my all-time favorites. If more people were as honest about their feelings as he was, mediation would be more like entertainment and less like work.

The power of agreement

This book would not be complete without a discussion of the tremendous flow of energy that is released when a conflict is resolved. It's immeasurable; it's euphoric; it's exhilarating; and it's empowering. When two minds meet and reach agreement, there is a tremendous release of pressure combined with a sense of accomplishment in having removed obstacles to harmony. I'm not talking just about mediated settlements. The power of agreement and the euphoria it generates is detectable in any situation in which two people disagree even on the most mundane issues. Naturally, its intensity is a factor of the magnitude of the disagreement, but it's a sensation that often goes unnoticed. It works within those who know it and facilitates the will to resolve every subsequent disagreement they encounter.

Let's say a husband and a wife are negotiating their lifestyle choices—for example, their taste in furniture. She likes contemporary; he likes early American. Early American wins. She may have given in because she doesn't care or because she doesn't care to argue. Depending on the negotiation style of the couple, this could be either good or bad. If she gave in because she's genuinely ambivalent about furniture, giving in works without resentment. Her views may carry the day in another area—child rearing or buying a car, for example. But if her husband wins every disagreement, there's an imbalance of power that could erode the basis of a healthy relationship. If the wife gives in with the intent of getting even in another way, that can work against the relationship as well.

But when two people come to an agreement without strings attached, the relationship is empowered by the resolution. We're not talking about one spouse converting the other's tastes over to become theirs, but coming to some agreement in which they can both find genuine satisfaction. If the wife can communicate openly, for example, and feel free to say "Lets do Early American in this room and Contemporary in that one," or "I don't care about furniture, but I do care about the kind of car I'd like us to have, so if you want to do the whole house in Early American, that's okay, but when we buy a car, we buy a sports car instead of a van," the couple has the skills to negotiate their way to harmony. When the wills of two people are mutually transformed into the will of the couple as one, their agreement takes on a power of its own that's greater than the sum of its parts. What's left is the satisfying of an innate inner desire to cooperate for the greater good.

Even though the power of agreement affects one's inner peace in relatively innocuous situations, this feeling is never more enriching than when people advance from antagonistic positions. When you bring two people from a point of separateness all the way to an agreement—especially if it's mutual and voluntary—there is an incredible sense of power generated internally for all involved. That's why mediated agreements are so successful. We just don't get that sense of empowerment when judges hand down decisions; we can't have that inner peace if we let our conflicts go unresolved; we'll never know that euphoria if intimidation is our method of dispute resolution; and we don't deserve to feel the power of agreement if we think violence will resolve our disputes.

A word of caution: this feeling of euphoria doesn't come with every resolution. Some new mediators, after facilitating a blissful "warm fuzzy" conclusion, come to expect the euphoria. Then it begins to drive the session toward a resolution instead of letting it happen. Novice mediators anticipating the intoxicating effect of a resolution soon try to create the feeling in cases that don't generate it naturally. This is counter to the process and can lead the mediator to become so hungry for the euphoric resolution that it takes on a higher priority than the resolution itself. It's a good way to scuttle the process.

Don't be driven by your own desire to resolve the conflict in a way that prompts hugs and tears of joy to flow like maple syrup over Niagara. When the feeling of euphoria comes with a resolution, rejoice in it; when it doesn't, appreciate the successful conclusion to the conflict and move on.

In mediation, the euphoria often comes at the end of the session. Sometimes it's a quiet euphoria, but you can feel it in the room. Some cases reach this point earlier in the process than in others. It could happen when feelings are expressed or at the very beginning when the facts are clarified. The whole dispute may fall away and the resolution clicks right into place. Or it may not happen until the terms of the agreement become clear. Then the animosity peels off like poorly glued veneer. It's an incredibly powerful, unifying experience and feeds the soul in a way that only those who facilitate harmony will ever know.

Section 4:
Applications for Mediation

Can't we all just get along?
—Rodney King

Mediation in the Work Place

Armed with the tools of mediation outlined in this book, anyone, regardless of their position within their organization, can mediate simple and moderately complex disputes. When incorporated into an organization's grievance policy, mediation gives employers and employees an option that permits them to resolve disputes that arise within the organization in a way that reduces or eliminates the animosity that can interfere with productive employee/employer relationships. It allows the disputants to resolve their conflict themselves and return to a working climate of cooperation instead of mutual suspicion and distrust. With mediation, companies and employees can get on with the business of their business to their mutual benefit.

Installing a mediation policy in the work place

When we talk about introducing mediation into the workplace we're talking about a process that begins with human resource (HR) managers. In companies that are too small to have a designated human resource department, the process begins with the individual who oversees company policies—a manager, owner or president of the company.

Those who want mediation to be a formal option in resolving disputes in the work place should be familiar with their company's grievance procedure. Typically, a grievance procedure is a well-defined sequence of events beginning with the requirement that initiating employees approach their adversaries or their adversaries' supervisors and attempt to resolve the conflict before activating formal grievance procedures. By the time most conflicts reach this first step, however, most employees will have already discussed their dispute with their adversaries and/or supervisor(s) or are too uncomfortable to do so. They engage the formal grievance procedure after they've taken all the initiative they can on their own. Any formal grievance procedure should include this first step to make sure the process is not activated before an employee's own attempts to resolve the conflict are exhausted.

The next step in most existing grievance procedures is usually requesting the initiating employee to make a formal, written complaint or a request for a conflict to be addressed by a grievance committee. This step initiates a lengthy process that involves selecting a grievance committee consisting of neutral employees or HR representatives who assemble, embark on an in-depth fact-finding process, question each disputant, interview witnesses and reassemble to deliberate a resolution. This procedure, however, unnecessarily bogs down the resolution process by taking an inordinate amount of time. Color it cumbersome.

It doesn't take a Ph.D. to realize that the process invites failure. Think about it. Initiating employees, having exhausted their attempts to resolve a dispute on their own, file a formal request with the HR department for a grievance committee hearing—a review by a committee that doesn't even exist yet (they are often not assembled until the need arises). HR managers notify upper management teams, construct a committee of willing and unbiased peers and send them out to gather facts by interviewing all those involved in the conflict—disputants and witnesses alike. They reassemble, compare the results of their findings (and hope they don't get conflicting accounts), construct a list of resolutions and concur on a recommended course of action that neither disputant may find acceptable. Regardless of whether either or both find the recommendations of the grievance committee acceptable, the president of the company may trash the entire outcome, throwing the conflict back to square one. It's hard to understand how employees would have much faith that their conflicts would be resolved fairly with so many obstacles.

In the time it takes to lumber through all the steps of a standard grievance procedure, conflicts have plenty of time to get worse. Given enough time, the unresolved conflict can weld the disputants to their point of view making them inflexible in accepting resolutions. Time also allows the disputants to campaign for allies, sabotage the process, polarize the work force, poison company or office morale and generally wreak havoc on the company. The resultant cold war could spark other conflicts, each in turn duplicating the negative effects of the first or launching another formal grievance. By inserting the mediation option *before* a grievance committee is assembled, the resolution of the conflict becomes more imminent.

I want to emphasize that it is essential to word the insertion of mediation into a company's grievance protocol in such a way so that it is to be considered an *option*. Companies can get into big trouble if they mandate that certain conflicts, or all conflicts for that matter, go to mediation. Dictating mediation over a more public form of dispute resolution subjects a company to all sorts of accusations, none of them flattering. Managers could be accused of covering up illegal or unethical practices, squelching whistle blowers, denying employees due process—the list is endless, especially if the press finds out. To avoid this pitfall, a company should state in its dispute resolution protocol that mediation is an option to be used at the discretion of the HR representative or other manager and with the consent of the disputants.

Also, take care to state in the mediation policy that participants will not be penalized for not reaching an agreement; nor would they be penalized for opting out of mediation. Use an experienced mediation consultant to help you establish the mediation policies and procedures and assist in the training of your company's mediators. Depending on the nature of the dispute, human resource managers and businesspersons need to know which disputes to mediate with a trained internal mediator and which to refer to a professional external mediator. The rule of thumb is simple:

If the dispute is between an employee and the company, give the employee the option to refer the dispute to an outside, external mediator; if the conflict is between two employees or between an employee and an immediate supervisor, offer the services of a trained, neutral, internal mediator unless the conflict is too sensitive or complex for the internal mediator to mediate with confidence.

Using an internal mediator

Resolving conflicts between two employees or groups of employees with an internal, trained mediator is one of the most savvy uses of mediation today. It just makes sense. I feel this application of mediation can benefit more people than any other and is, by and large, the main reason I wanted to make this manual available. The dispute between Lucia and Hernandez that we have been guiding through the mediation process is an excellent example of the kind of dispute that managers, supervisors and HR administrators can help resolve before it dismantles the morale and productivity of a department or an entire company.

Examples of the types of conflicts internal mediators can effectively manage include:

- *interpersonal disputes (e.g., job responsibilities, scheduling conflicts, departmental policy, smoking/personal hygiene conflicts, work space/territorial disputes, etc.)*
- *simple racial discrimination disputes*
- *simple sex discrimination cases*
- *simple benefits and compensation conflicts*

A dispute that lends itself well to internal mediation is one in which both parties feel the internal mediator would be impartial and under no pressure to urge one resolution over another. Let's say one of your senior salespersons files a grievance against her immediate supervisor that she was passed up for assignment to a preferred sales territory because of her sex. Based on some of his statements, she claims that her supervisor, a male, is of the opinion that the clients in that particular territory would respond better to (translated: buy more from) a male sales representative. This type of conflict is perfect for an internal mediator. It is also a dispute that is not beyond the level of expertise, experience, and confidence of the internal mediator. When these criteria are met, a quick and confidential resolution is possible with an internal mediator.

What to look for in an internal mediator

In drafting mediation into the grievance protocol, architects of the policy need to consider who they want to choose and train as mediators. Options include:

- *employee relations staff*
- *HR managers or their staff*
- *managers*
- *supervisors*

Regardless of who is in the pool of potential mediators, there should be a sufficient number trained so that all potential disputants will feel their cases will be handled fairly and by an unbiased individual. It is their perception of fairness that is important in achieving a lasting resolution.

If disputants see that the mediator chosen for their case is part of the problem or has ties to their adversary, there will be a reluctance to enter into mediation. If the manager closest to the dispute feels comfortable mediating the dispute and both parties accept that person as their mediator, the decision of who mediates is easy. If either of the disputants or the mediator is uncomfortable with the assignment, the manager would do well to choose another trained, in-house mediator to handle the dispute. If the dispute is between managers or supervisors, the mediator of choice would be a HR representative or an upper level manager.

As discussed at length earlier, good mediators are compassionate, good listeners and good communicators. It would behoove readers serious about implementing a mediation program in their organization or company to refer to Section 3, *Qualities of a successful mediator,* when it comes time to select those within the organization who are to be trained in the skills of mediation. Once willing employees are recruited and trained to mediate, the mediation protocol can become part of the company's grievance policy.

Using an external mediator

Not all conflicts are best served by internal mediation. Whenever the use of an internal mediator challenges the perception of neutrality for either disputing party, or when a conflict is too sensitive or complex for an internal mediator, an outside mediator should be contracted. Examples of the types of disputes that warrant external mediators include:

- *wrongful termination claims*
- *complex racial discrimination claims*
- *complex sex discrimination claims*
- *worker's compensation*
- *complex benefits and compensation disputes*
- *sexual harassment*
- *vendor disputes*
- *third-party disputes*

APPLICATIONS FOR MEDIATION

- *consumer/customer complaints*
- *debt/collections issues*
- Americans with Disabilities Act *violations*
- *complex* Family Leave Act *violations*

Companies benefit when such conflicts are contracted to outside mediators. When an issue is resolved outside the company, the organization is shielded from the details of the case. Since mediation is a confidential process and the parties agree not to use anything said in the session in later hearings or legal actions, companies remain unaware of all that transpires except the resolution. By staying out of the fray, they remain happily oblivious to certain revelations that they may otherwise be forced to address. In addition, companies are open to accusations of improper procedural errors when they mediate internally. By contracting complicated, sensitive cases to an outside mediator, those who know the difference between simple and complex cases eliminate the risk of an internal mediator mishandling the case. Whenever a company is interested in reducing its exposure to these risks, an outside mediator provides a valuable service.

But the disputants can benefit from outside mediation as well. Let's look at sexual harassment disputes as a prime example. Besides being beyond the expertise of the casual mediator, managers who offer external mediation as an option to the targets of sexual harassment give those involved the opportunity to have their concerns addressed without the public exposure that formal charges can bring.

Often, the desire to pursue a formal process to stop sexual harassment comes after an employee's own attempts to repel the offensive behavior have been ineffective. In the early stages, targets of sexual harassment are not so much interested in publicizing the offensive behavior as they are in wanting the behavior to stop. It is during this phase that mediation is most effective. Although, traditionally, upper-level managers have dictated how sexual harassment cases should be handled, when they make mediation the preferred option, they demonstrate a willingness to allow the target and the alleged offender to determine the arena in which the conflict should be resolved. Even though targets may initially bristle at the prospect of facing their adversary in a mediation setting, other approaches to the problem would clearly be more difficult, destructive, time-consuming and emotionally draining to all parties.

Having their sexual harassment cases mediated will not appeal to everyone who is offended by another's unsolicited advances or suggestive remarks and gestures. If the company or organization is suspected of downplaying the complaint or attempting to protect the offender, mediation may not be an appealing option to the target. It may appear to the target that in offering mediation the company is trying to keep the dispute a secret. Neither would mediation be considered an option if the target of sexual harassment is after a financial windfall or the deep personal satisfaction that would come in taking the case to a more public arena. Lastly, if the target no longer wants to work for the organization, urging a mediated settlement will take a good bit of persuasion.

To dispel fears that the company would trivialize the charges, mediation should be offered to targeted employees as an option when they first bring their complaint to the attention of the human resource department or to a member of the management team. Likewise, it is equally important for offenders to be approached with mediation as an option rather than as a requirement. Without giving them the mediation option, they could claim that the company forced mediation upon them or denied them certain rights to due process. If the offenders are offered mediation as a way to face the problem—i.e., to share control over the outcome, to hear a first-hand account of how their behavior affects their target, and

APPLICATIONS FOR MEDIATION

to have the opportunity to interact more appropriately as alternatives to a reprimand, sanction or termination—the mediation option should have great appeal.

Another example of a dispute that requires an external mediator would be a worker's compensation claim against the company. For example, let's say your company manufactures specialized parts for the auto industry. One of your newest employees quickly masters a complex piece of equipment. Last week, however, he claimed that he suffers from a repetitive stress injury which has now manifested itself as carpel tunnel syndrome. He has lost productivity, can't perform his function at work without a great deal of pain and suggests your worker's compensation insurance should pay for lost wages and medical treatment.

You reject his request because you know he bowls six nights a week, and you claim his injury is a result of his recreational activity. Still, you hate to lose him because he's as familiar with the equipment as he is the seven-ten split. Since replacing him means spending thousands of dollars recruiting and training someone to work the equipment, you'd like to keep him if possible. He knows that the only other company that could employ his skills is in Bangladesh, so he'd like to work out a resolution, too. This is the type of scenario that begs to be mediated. Still, if you or a representative from your company were to offer to mediate a resolution, the mediator would not seem to the employee to be neutral. Since this dispute is against the company instead of an individual, an outside mediator will be the only type of mediator that would be seen as neutral to both parties.

Likewise, disputes involving former employees necessitate the use of an external mediator. Say, for example, that after quitting her job, an employee finds that she has not been compensated for a week's worth of vacation time that had accumulated before she left the company in good standing. Numerous discussions with the payroll manager and human resources representatives have not resolved the conflict. Feeling that she has been cheated out of a week's vacation, she's pursuing legal channels to recover what your policy manual says is rightly hers. No mediator within that organization is going to appear to the former employee to be without bias. Unless an outside mediator is secured, the determined former employee will move the conflict into another arena, one that will be undoubtedly more costly and time consuming for both parties.

What to look for in an external mediator

When a conflict is best served by an external mediator, look for a mediator the same way you look for an auto mechanic: someone who has experience, training, and who leaves a trail of satisfied customers. Ask about experience. Ask about certification. Some states, courts, and jurisdictions certify mediators. If your external mediator has certification, that's good; if not, it isn't necessarily a sign that he or she is a second-rate mediator, but that certification might not be available in your area. Since mediation is relatively new, the norm is for mediators to have only a few of years of experience. However, mediators with 10 to 20 years of experience do exist.

Let me state that in having trained well over a thousand mediators, I'm convinced that there is no correlation between one's educational level or the number of hours of training one's had and being a good mediator. Rather, it seems to be a matter of personal disposition, i.e., philosophical orientation toward conflict coupled with experience, that translates into mediation skill.

Find out what types and numbers of conflicts they've mediated, where they trained and what models of mediation they use. If they don't understand that last item, find someone else because they are either self taught or not taught at all. Their answer should be one of the types I discuss in Section 3, *Creating a favorable mediation environment*.

Record keeping

All mediated conflicts should be well documented. Records should be maintained with regard to every conflict's resolution. All grievance records should show if mediation was offered and if so, that it was offered as an option. Remember that the actual notes from the session itself should be destroyed, but the final resolution agreement should be kept on file for referral, follow-up and to protect against a challenge to the agreement. The final disposition of all disputes, whether mediated internally, externally or resolved some other way, should be retrievable. Written records also track a conflict's history should it erupt again. Nevertheless, to protect the integrity of mediation as a confidential process, the records maintained should not include the mediator's notes or identify either party as being unwilling to agree to a resolution. Only the written agreement and/or the notations of the referral should be maintained.

Mediation in Schools

One of the most inspiring applications of mediation I've seen evolve in the years I've been mediating is in teaching the students of our community school systems the skills to mediate conflicts between their peers. Nowhere else is mediation better suited; nowhere else can it give youth the tools they need in the formative years to resolve the disputes they will encounter throughout their adult lives; and nowhere else can mediation satisfy an organization's mission statement as often and as successfully as it can in an educational institution. In this section we will look at internal and external mediation within school systems and learn how a peer/mediation program can process the vast majority of conflicts that arise in a school setting.

Internal mediation

More than ten thousand student/peer mediation programs are functioning today across the United States. Children as young as third and fourth graders are being taught mediation skills. In lower grades, some schools provide an education curriculum that prepares students for mediation in the later grades. Some elementary schools even give selected students T-shirts that say "conflict manager," and let them mediate fights and disputes as they arise on the playground. I have heard an account of one teacher who overheard a playground conversation in which students were debating the recess activity. After an impasse was reached, one student suggested that first they play softball, and then they play kickball. So the language of negotiation can be learned and effectively employed at an early age.

Young people seem to be natural mediators. I was fortunate enough once to view the taping of an *ABC World News Tonight* segment on peer mediation in schools. It involved several middle school students mediating a dispute between a couple of other students. They did an excellent job, and I was thoroughly convinced that children can be better new mediators than adults. Adults tend to play the role of therapist or attorney when they first learn the process; kids just mediate. They are much more streamlined about it and more natural.

Students are remarkably capable and eager to be given the power to resolve disputes among their own. In student/peer mediation programs, students are taught the skills to mediate conflicts in which other students are directly involved. By empowering them with these skills, administrators give students the authority to resolve disputes among their peers instead of sending conflicts through the traditional channels. Admittedly, this reshuffles the hierarchy of power that has been in place for generations, but family counselors will tell you that if young people are not given some control over their lives, they will wrestle it away. Giving students the opportunity to resolve disputes among themselves demonstrates a trust in their ability to become responsible for an outcome formerly mandated by authority figures. When we relinquish a little authority to students, the message they receive is that we perceive them to be mature enough to handle a responsibility traditionally kept to ourselves and other adult authorities. To students, this empowerment has a tremendously positive impact. Students feel more as a part of the educational process. They feel more trusted and worthy of the confidence given them. When given a chance to take on this kind of adult responsibility, rarely will they fail to impress.

In giving students these "keys to the car" so to speak, student mediators not only sense a trust in their ability to resolve conflicts that arise among them in a school setting but learn the language of negotiation for themselves. It is a language they will find invaluable when they leave school for the larger social environment they will inhabit throughout their adult lives. For most students, if they are not empowered with the skills of alternative dispute resolution in this setting, they may never encounter the opportunity again.

Student/peer mediation programs are best suited to resolve the same types of disputes that are best served by mediation in the work place and the community: interpersonal conflicts ("he-said-she-said" and boyfriend/girlfriend issues are among the most popular), property damage disputes and some scuffles that do not involve serious injury. Examples of conflicts that students could be trained to mediate include:

- *One student accuses another of irreparably damaging his science fair display and demands compensation;*
- *A conflict between two students over a preferred parking spot is escalating beyond threats;*

- *One student is accused of stealing another's property from a locker;*
- *A student insists on eating her Limburger cheese sandwich in the cafeteria with the rest of the students every day, the stench forcing droves to the vending machines instead where they become riotous for the limited supply of Twinkies and chips.*

Installing internal mediation

Without mediation, a school's disciplinary measures are limited to detention, suspension, expulsion, parent conferences, and maybe a good scolding. Some school systems still even include paddling as a disciplinary technique. But today, with mediation as a tool, administrators can now go beyond the traditional disciplinary actions to a more positive, productive approach.

Since guidance counselors and principals are so overburdened, I don't categorically recommend that their responsibilities include implementing and maintaining a student/peer mediation program. However, they are probably in the best position to initiate and oversee the program. Certainly, if there is a teacher committed to the establishment of the program, I would recruit that individual as the overseer. Parents enthusiastic about the concept can also be excellent sponsors in conjunction with a faculty member. Coupled with a supportive member of the teaching staff, a parent-teacher team can give the program all the momentum it needs to get off the ground and stay aloft.

The sponsor of a student/peer mediation group first needs to solicit the blessings of the administration and possibly the school board to begin constructing the program. Some will be receptive, some won't; it depends on a multitude of factors from individual orientation to a regional acceptance of progressive concepts. For example, schools that adhere to the more traditional educational philosophies will be more resistant to student/peer mediation than schools that explore progressive innovations in education.

Nevertheless, once a student/peer mediation program is approved, sponsors should carry the banner of mediation and recruit the support of their colleagues. Educating the students, teachers, and administrators on the benefits, methods, and steps to implementing a student/peer mediation program is as simple as distributing informational material and engaging in formal and informal discussions whenever the opportunities arise.

To successfully implement a student/peer mediation program several details are important. They include forming an alliance with a community mediation program, establishing the mediation protocol, good record keeping, careful selection of student mediators and effective communication among all connected with the student/peer mediation program.

Community mediator support

A good student/peer mediation program has a strong link to an established community mediation service. Establish a healthy relationship with a community mediator who can provide initial and follow-up training and who is willing to stay committed to a partnership with the school system in maintaining the student/peer mediation program. Some community mediation programs have volunteer mediators who are eager to assist in establishing and maintaining peer mediation programs in schools.

Establishing the mediation protocol

Prepare a written protocol for activating the mediation process. Just as in interjecting the mediation option into a company's grievance protocol, schools need to insert the mediation option into their policy records and student handbooks. A mediation program that no one knows about is not a mediation program.

It must function to thrive and it must be publicized to function. The school's community mediation sponsor can assist in establishing this policy.

A student interested in activating the mediation process should first fill out a brief referral form that describes the nature of the conflict and identifies the other disputant(s). The program coordinator then must initiate the mediation process just as I have discussed earlier in the *How conflicts come to mediation* section. Document what types of conflicts the student/peer program will mediate since not all conflicts that arise in school settings, as in community and business environments, lend themselves to internal mediation. We will discuss these exceptions later under *external mediation*.

Student mediator selection

In selecting student mediators, get a good cross-section of the student body. Typically, the knee-jerk response to selecting student mediators is for administrators of the program to select students who show leadership abilities in sports, academic or social arenas. By doing so, the opportunity to impact the student who really needs to learn how to manage conflict (especially their own) is missed. By picking students who are disruptive, acting out or basic trouble makers, you are choosing those who know what conflict is all about. Nobody will benefit more. I've heard of some inspiring stories of "bad apple" students excelling in this process and taking pride in being mediators. Most of the disruptive students are looking for attention, ways to be noticed. Giving them the opportunity to be mediators gives them a very positive way to be noticed in an arena with which they are very familiar.

Communication

Quarterly meetings with student mediators are important to maintain the lines of communication between the mediators, the sponsors, the community mediation organization and the school administrators. These meetings would disseminate information on the number of requests for mediation that were filed, cases that were referred to other avenues, cases that resulted in mediation sessions and the number of successful sessions.

Record keeping

Good records are essential to the success and longevity of a peer mediation program. I'm not talking about the actual dialogues of the mediation sessions themselves—those notes should be discarded—but copies of contracts and records of disputes and their outcomes constitute an overall good case management system and should be detailed and readily accessible. But not to everyone. Records should be maintained with strict confidentiality to protect the identities of participants and the nature of the disputes. You should establish a clear policy to limit the availability of records to principals, mediation support person(s), and administrators. Students who have taken their disputes through the student/peer mediation program should also have access to the records of their case. The mediation file should contain:

- *requests for mediation*—each request for mediation should be kept on file even if the dispute is resolved on its own. These written records will track the history of a conflict should it erupt again;
- *cases that resulted in mediation sessions* keeping track of the conflicts mediated by the peer group is critical from an organizational standpoint and becomes essential to keep the cases moving toward resolution;
- **sessions results**—records of the outcome of each peer-mediated session should not be a *he-said-this-she-said-that* transcript, but a written summary of the session results. The actual signed contracts are essential for follow-up compliance and to document the agreement in the case of future

contradictions. When the dispute has been resolved, the written, signed resolution is all that is kept as a permanent record;
- **cases that were referred to other avenues**—not all referrals for a peer-mediated resolution are best served by mediation. Some cases may need to be referred to the school administration or even law enforcement or probation authorities.

External mediation.

Designated mediation program managers should not attempt to activate student/peer mediation for all conflicts. Some require the use of outside mediators. The astute school mediation proponent needs to know the difference. Basically, when the conflict involves anyone other than students, student/peer mediation is not appropriate. For example:

- *student/teacher disputes*
- *student/administration disputes*
- *teacher/teacher disputes*
- *teacher/administration disputes*
- *parent/teacher disputes*
- *parent/administration disputes*

These disputes are best handled by professional mediators to assure neutrality. If a school tried to use an internal mediator to handle a school vandalism case, there would be a partiality involved. Trained, volunteer community mediators are well-equipped to handle these types of disputes.

External mediation can be a tool for restitution as well as healing. I once mediated a high school vandalism case in which the vandals and the school authorities worked out restitution for $10,000 in damages to the gymnasium. This was offered as an

APPLICATIONS FOR MEDIATION

alternative to having a detached judge affix retribution—one that suited the judge more than the school—and would probably have been beyond what was realistic for the offenders to meet.

The session was held in the school and included representatives from administration, the teachers, parents and student body— all who felt victimized. Allowing for a mediated settlement in this case served several purposes. First, it literally brought the offenders back to the scene of the crime. Secondly, it produced an agreement on compensation the offenders could realistically provide—a partial payment and an agreement to work off the balance in services to the school. Thirdly, it put the victims and the offenders together to work out a mutually acceptable form of compensation instead of a court-mandated payment. Lastly, it gave the members of the school community an opportunity to confront these boys, and let them know how it affected them and how violated they felt. All these facilitated the healing process and worked to provide lasting impressions that went a lot further than court-ordered restitution would have in deterring a repeat offense.

In selecting outside mediators, the qualities to look for are the same that a business manager would look for as I discussed in that section under *What to look for in an external mediator.*

Other Applications

Therapists and mediation

At times, a fine line exists between psychotherapy and mediation. Psychotherapists deal primarily with internal conflicts, those that arise *within* an individual. However, therapists who know when and how to apply the techniques of mediation to address *external* conflicts will find that the internal conflicts become more easily addressed. For example, let's say a husband lost his wife's car in a poker game. (I know this is trite, but bear with me for the sake of example. If it helps, substitute "wife's car" with any other coveted possession and "poker game" with any other setting that provokes such acts of spontaneous stupidity.) Not only does she have to take the bus to work, but the entire marriage has been thrown into jeopardy because of his bone-headed gamble. They seek a marriage therapist. (Lucky for him; she should have thrown the bum out.)

The therapist realizes that there are two problems to address. The first, and most immediate problem, is that the wife wants and needs her transportation returned or replaced. Secondly, the underlying problem(s) that allowed the incident to take place have to be explored and eradicated if the marriage is to survive. In cases like this, without resolving whatever external conflict clouds the surface, therapists aren't able to get to the underlying causes of a dysfunctional relationship. When therapists *mediate* to clear away the immediate conflict, they can then *counsel* to unearth the thought processes that allow disputes to arise in the first place. The value of mediation to therapists, therefore, is to stabilize relationships before or during therapy.

But there are pitfalls.

• Therapists must know the difference between therapy and mediation in order to use them in synergy. The two techniques are designed for different outcomes. Therapy resolves inner conflict so that individuals can cope, evolve and adapt; mediation helps resolve external conflicts so that people can constructively resolve disputes with others. Although both share the goal of reducing inner turmoil, therapy is a much more complex process and one that mediation will never pretend to mimic. When used to clear the surface clutter of an external conflict, mediation can make it easier to apply therapy.

• Therapists should never mediate a conflict in which they cannot be impartial. Therapists cannot effectively mediate if only one of the disputants is a client. Not only does the therapist break the impartiality requirement, but the other disputant will recognize the imbalance of power. In these cases, an outside mediator should be sought.

• Therapists who utilize mediators to facilitate the removal of surface conflicts so that they can more easily extract the internal processes that they need to address must be up front with clients. Inform them that the immediate conflict has to be addressed before the root causes of their anxiety can be tackled. Stress that the mediation process is only to facilitate therapy, not replace it, and that the session might render a lessening of hostilities. Explain that mediation is not designed to address the them, won't lead to a long term solution to underlying problems, nor facilitate the depth of understanding and change of attitudes that can lead to long term changes of behavior. Don't let on, however, that sometimes mediation is all it takes to kick a couple back onto a functional mode of interaction.

Let's say that a couple seeks therapy because the wife, who has been assigned the traditional spousal roles, rebels against living the type of lifestyle her mother had in shouldering the domestic responsibilities. She's never discussed it with her husband, though, and now it is affecting every aspect of their relationship. She sleeps on the couch, washes only her clothes, cooks only what he hates, and speaks only when she has to. The tension is unbearable for them both yet the real issue still has not been discussed. He talks her into seeing a marriage therapist together. During the very first session the wife unloads. Right then is where the therapist should stop being a therapist and start being a mediator. This is not the time to propose solutions, but rather let the participants construct one for themselves. The therapist should follow the steps of mediation I've discussed. Have each explain their conflict, vent their emotions and tell each other what they want out of the relationship. Sometimes it's this simple; sometimes it's not. But if the therapist sees that the nature of the problem is strictly behavioral, mediating the conflict might be all that's necessary.

This example underscores the importance of getting to the surface conflicts first. If conflicts like we have just seen exist, they should be unveiled and addressed in the first session or two—long before you spend too much time trying to drum up deeper causes.

Attorneys and mediation

Attorneys build their careers around ways to drive conflicts toward resolution. Traditionally, however, their approach has employed adversarial alternatives. When the mediation option came along it broadened the attorney's spectrum of options with litigation at one end and mediation at the other. Favoring litigation as the option of choice in this spectrum is not so much a reflection on the nature of attorneys as it is of society's antagonistic reaction to conflict as I've discussed earlier. Some attorneys are, of course, advocates of themselves and their incomes more so than for their client's best interests. Those attorneys will continue to milk the litigation process to maximize their own gains. Those attorneys who would read this book are not among them.

I hasten to add that many conflicts do actually belong in court. In others, the disputants are predisposed to litigation. Sometimes society at large actually benefits from the publicity that litigation generates. However, many other cases don't belong in litigation, yet are steered in that direction for a multitude of personal, professional or political reasons. On balance, however, mediation offers just as many personal, professional and societal benefits as does litigation and probably more. Attorneys who look at a conflict and consider all the options available for its resolution instead of only those pathways that involve the courts and individual interests benefit in many ways:

APPLICATIONS FOR MEDIATION

- *They spend less time on cases in which their representation is nominally influential;*
- *They have more time to represent those clients whose cases demand of all of their resources;*
- *They can expand the services they offer to include a multitude of dispute resolution techniques, including mediation, not just the most adversarial;*
- *They are seen in the community as a broad-based dispute resolution service that can steer the community's conflicts toward the most appropriate method for each individual conflict;*
- *They serve the community by offering an alternative form of dispute resolution that facilitates healing within the community instead of adversity;*
- *By guiding the disputes their clients bring them toward a less adversarial pathway, they lessen the burden of anxiety that they must bear when orchestrating a dispute through channels that are adversarial by nature.*

When the nature of the conflict demands a legal recourse, attorneys are well suited to pursue a legal action for their clients. However, clients and judges who insist restitution be paid for damages incurred as a direct result of a criminal act will find mediation to be a perfectly legitimate arena in which to facilitate closure and healing. For this purpose and many others, mediation offers attorneys a superlative antidote to the animosity that descends upon those embroiled in bitter interpersonal conflicts.

Attorneys can utilize mediation in two ways: by applying the techniques of mediation as part of their legal services and by referring cases to professional mediators.

Attorneys as mediators

Attorneys who offer this less antagonistic approach to dispute resolution can find their careers to be more personally and professionally rewarding than those who muscle as many conflicts into the court room as they can. What kind of attorney makes a good mediator?

- *Attorneys who are tired of the adversarial nature of their work;*
- *Attorneys whose temperament is not well-suited for antagonistic processes;*
- *Attorneys who don't believe that the adversarial process always leads to the best solution;*
- *Attorneys who are philosophically in tune with the underlying principles of mediation (empowernment of the individuals to resolve their own problems, the importance of good and open communication between parties to dispute resolution, etc.);*
- *Lawyers attuned to cooperation and dedicated to eliminating lingering animosity.*

Attorneys who want to mediate should be careful not to let legal thinking sneak its way into the mediation process—namely, the tendency to project a specific outcome and then proceed to facilitate it and the desire to have one's opinion heard. There's nothing wrong with attorneys envisioning an outcome, but facilitating their own preconceived outcome robs the disputants of one of the greatest benefits of mediation: the opportunity to become the architects of the resolution.

As mediators, it is imperative that attorneys allow the disputants to engineer the outcome as much as possible. It helps to bear in mind that *all that matters is that the conflict is resolved satisfactorily in the eyes of the disputants*. The tendency, however, is for attorneys to panic when an emerging outcome is not perceived to be "fair" to one of the disputants and that that person could do much better in a court room. The attorney-turned-mediator allows the disputants to come to whatever agreement they can both accept regardless of whether or not the resolution is "fair" in that attorney's opinion. If the conflict is resolved to the satisfaction of both parties, the conflict is resolved. Period. Providing there are no violations of the law involved, the attorney has succeeded and has reason to rejoice in the victory with just as much pride as if he or she had won a multi-million dollar settlement. The healing facilitated is worth at least as much.

In court, attorneys speak on their client's behalf. Their opinions, conjectures, objections, motions, suppositions, petitions, accusations and suggestions are all recorded and heavily influence the outcome. In mediation, however, these serve only to derail the process. Being put in a role where one's opinions are irrelevant can be very frustrating. Some attorneys may find this a difficult transition to make. But attorney-mediators must make the maintenance of the mediation process their only priority. If they do not adhere to the process, try to muscle an outcome, dictate a solution under the guise of mediation or start serving their own or a disputant's interests, they are no longer mediating. Knowing this tendency exists is all most attorneys need to know to keep it from interfering with their ability to mediate successfully.

Most attorneys who are predisposed to the principles of mediation, who want to do more than usher a conflict toward a legal resolution, who want to address the interpersonal damages that conflict brings, find that mediation will meet their needs. Those lawyers I know who have incorporated mediation into their practices have found it to be a rewarding and refreshing break from the adversarial posturing they usually have to take. Some have even forsaken the adversarial approach completely and rebuilt their practices around mediation.

Attorneys referring conflicts to mediation

Every time attorneys are approached by potential clients with a possible case, they evaluate its merit and decide whether or not to advance it toward the legal arena. The factors that contribute to this decision are complex, numerous and different for each attorney. Mediation not only clears an attorney's case load of frivolous lawsuits, but facilitates the most amenable resolutions that situations and dispositions allow. It also teaches people how to resolve disputes with a minimum of hostility and negativism. More than any other professional, attorneys are in a position to channel conflicts toward constructive resolutions. No one is better placed to assess mediation's potential to bring disputes to mutually satisfying conclusions.

Victim/offender mediation

Victim-offender (V/O) mediation programs offer the legal system a viable supplement or even alternative to traditional forms of punishment. In V/O mediation, victims and offenders meet in the presence of a mediator to facilitate restitution or reparation. Even though mediation must be secondary to the legal process in cases that involve violations of the law, V/O mediation allows the parties to work toward compensation for the offense and to facilitate healing.

Many argue that exposing offenders to victims, and therefore to the human cost of their transgressions, is a better deterrent to a repeat offense than jail time. Most cases involve young or first offenders who commit property crimes such as vandalism, theft or more severe offenses. An example of one such case is that of a drunk driver who caused a fatal accident that killed a volunteer fire fighter. The court ordered him into mediation with the family of the victim. The session generated an agreement between the family and the offender that the offender obtain training as a fire fighter and serve a number of years on the volunteer fire department in place of the victim. Granted, this type of agreement would not be possible or even desirable in all similar situations, but in this case would jail time have been a better deterrent to a repeat offense? I don't think so.

Often a judge may order the offender to participate in mediated restitution or reparation to the victim. For example, if a drunk driver ended up on your neighbor's meticulously groomed lawn and sank up to his axles, he could not only suffer the legal consequences of driving under the influence of alcohol, but he could be ordered to mediate *restitution* to his victim—to return the property back to the way it was. If you had learned the skills of mediation and were trained as a mediator, you could help the victim and the offender come to an agreement on the repair of your neighbor's yard.

If the drunk driver killed your neighbor's champion irish setter instead of his fescue, you could be mediating *reparation*—compensation for an offense which resulted in consequences that cannot be reversed. In either case, victim/offender mediation is a valuable tool for courts that seek to compensate the victims of criminal acts rather than force a particular type of restitution upon the offender—a resolution that generates hostility whenever people don't have a say in the outcome.

Some types of assault cases—those that don't involve sexual, domestic or child assault—can be effectively served by mediation. Assaults by strangers—barroom brawls, random acts of violence, etc.—are often referred to mediation for restitution or reparation. All cases, however, that originate as criminal offenses must first be dealt with in accordance with the law before being sent to a formal victim/offender mediation program.

Other applications

Divorce cases. In no other type of dispute do emotions run as high as they do in divorce cases—all the more reason they should be mediated whenever possible. Since the outcome impacts the lives of the estranged couple so deeply and for the rest of their lives, they should make every attempt to become the architects of their dissolution. Child custody, visitation, child support, debt liability, the disbursement of jointly-owned property, etc. can be addressed successfully to the mutual satisfaction of divorcing spouses when a mediator is allowed to facilitate the process.

Mediation serves divorce cases so well that it's as if it were designed exclusively for settling divorce disputes alone. Because nothing is resolved in mediation without the approval of both parties, it allows divorcing couples to separate as amicably as the circumstances allow.

Disputes involving health care providers. All healthcare facilities—doctors' offices, hospitals, nursing homes, outpatient clinics, immediate care centers, visiting nurse associations,—struggle with the same types of disputes: sexual harassment, bill collection, malpractice, quality of care, employee grievances, etc. As it does for any industry, mediation offers an option to resolve customer (patient) disputes and employee conflicts to the mutual satisfaction of both parties. Malpractice and personal injury cases, although more complicated, can often come to mediated settlements after any legalities have been addressed. Mediation brings the parties together to vent their frustrations and generate resolutions that limit the expense of time and money.

In addition, as the healthcare industry continues its belt-tightening, insurance companies are challenging the tests and treatments that healthcare providers claim to be necessary for their patients. Healthcare providers can effectively employ mediation to facilitate resolutions with insurance carriers on the bills they submit on behalf of their patients.

Commercial disputes. Based on their low bid, a contracting company is awarded a contract to build a high school. Four years later, the school is only three-fourths complete, a year beyond the contracted completion date and $500,000 over the initial cost. The school corporation refuses to pay the additional half million and construction stops. Houston, we have a problem.

Both sides have much to lose if construction does not resume. Legal action could take years to force the school to pay and/or the contractor to finish, possibly leaving the school and contractor bankrupt. A mediator can bring the two together and facilitate a resolution before the two parties antagonize the conflict beyond repair.

Personal injury/property damage. Insurance companies know that if they aren't careful about how they handle their claims, court-awarded settlements can bury them. That's why the insurance industry is one of the biggest consumers of mediation. Who wins when insurance claims go to mediation instead of to trial? Usually all those involved.

Let's say Susan is driving her brother Martin to the dentist to have a root canal. Entering the same intersection is Ruppert, a stock market analyst who has most of his clients over-invested in blue chip stocks. Feeling very bullish, Ruppert is reading financial reports on the way to work and doesn't see that the light has changed. He slams into the quarter panel of Susan's '89 Yugo dislocating her shoulder and rendering the vehicle a total loss. Not only does he crash, but so do the blue chips later that day.

Weeks later, Ruppert's insurance company offers to settle for what Susan perceives to be an insulting pittance. Her Yugo cannot be repaired and her arm, although replaced in its socket in the emergency room, offers only a limited range of movement. Offended by their offer, she threatens to take the case to court. Upon hearing this, Ruppert hangs up the phone and looks longingly at the ledge outside his office window.

A month and several depositions later, Ruppert's insurance company calls Susan and offers to enter into mediation. When she accepts, the winners are well-defined. Susan wins because she gets more than the insurance company was willing to pay initially; she can now afford to lease a vehicle while she embarks upon an international quest to find another '89 Yugo; her medical bills are covered; she feels well compensated for her pain, which has completely subsided with physical therapy; and she won't spend the next three years in litigation. Ruppert wins because he isn't being sued by an obsessed Yugo-maniac who wants more for her vehicle than the insurance company's blue book suggests it's worth. His insurance company wins because the case won't got to trial with a jury that could possibly consist of the world's only other living Yugo-maniac. It could happen. Susan's brother, her lawyer, wins because he got more for his sister in the agreement than he thought he'd get and avoided the remote possibility that she would lose the case. Unfortunately, he's the only other casualty of the entire episode (besides the Yugo); he missed his appointment for his root canal and had to spend another week eating only those meals that could be poured from a blender.

Franchise disputes. Let's say you've finally reached your lifelong dream of owning an Arctic Monkey Frozen Banana franchise. When frozen bananas start selling like hotcakes (hey, stranger things have happened), so do the franchises. The parent company, Arctic Monkey, Inc., sells a franchise to another entrepreneur who plans on opening up his store three miles from yours. You find a clause in your franchise agreement that protects you from such competition and protest to the parent company. Mediation is perfect for this type of dispute or any other that may arise between franchisees and franchisors.

Suppose your franchise was in the Napa Valley and the parent company was in Louisville, Kentucky. How do you mediate with an adversary thousands of miles away? Video-conferencing is gradually linking people around the world, and mediation is a perfect application of the technology. A mediator simply orchestrates a mediation session to be conducted via the airwaves with this technology. In fact, the mediator might well be in a third location necessitating a three-way teleconference in which participants never physically meet or dwell in the same room. The mediator does the electronic leg work necessary to get the parties to agree to mediation and to set up the teleconference. At a preset time and date, the parties assemble at teleconference sites and go through the standard mediation procedures as if they were in the same room. If necessary, caucuses can also be conducted electronically. When a resolution is reached, the mediator faxes the proposed agreement for review and signatures. The next day, you can go on selling frozen bananas, hopefully without competition from another franchise.

This technique would work well with almost any dispute between franchisees and their franchisors. Mediation also holds promise for work place disputes that arise during the course of business, just as it does for all types of organizations.

Business partnerships. When partnerships are formed, the parties should agree on the terms of the partnership—how the profits are to be dispersed, how the risk is to be shared, who is responsible for what aspects of the business, etc. Mediation serves this necessity well and can be conducted by any neutral third party. Just as parties should agree on the terms of the creation of the partnership so too, should they consider the terms of its dissolution if misfortune negates their best efforts to succeed. Whether the business partners are friends with a business idea, physicians building a practice, family members opening up a store, etc., mediation offers partners and business associates the opportunity to protect their interests.

It's difficult for business partners to consider what to do with their collective assets in the event of failure while they are, at the same time, collaborating with confidence on strategies they hope will guarantee their success. Nevertheless, the levelheaded business partner knows that anything can happen to a market, a business, the economy and to a partnership and that one's interests in a partnership need to be protected. Not only should mediators make sure partners discuss the dispersal of the assets that the business generates but also the assets each partner brings into the relationship. They should agree upon the return, dispersal or compensation of those assets in writing in the event of a business or partnership failure.

Mediation can help by anticipating possible outcomes and devising a good exit plan for the partners. It can also be a valuable tool in negotiating the terms of a partnership dissolution for those who have not established a buy-out strategy and are suddenly faced with dissolution. The distribution of assets and assumption of liabilities can be successfully completed with mediation. Regardless, business partners should always consult an attorney before signing any dissolution agreement, even if it had been generated through mediation.

Often, mediating the terms of a potential business dissolution is nothing more than having a neutral third party document the terms of agreement that the business partners have accepted and making sure that the distribution of all assets and potential assets are considered. Anyone skilled in the techniques of mediation as described in this handbook can mediate these types of agreements. Indeed, they are among the easiest to mediate since, more than likely, the parties are already cooperative.

Product liability. Product liability lawsuits can create two situations that mediated resolutions cannot: 1) they can rain a downpour of publicity upon the corporation that created the product in question or delivered the disputed service; and 2) they can make the lawyers who take their share of what the jury awards very happy should they win for their client. If neither one of these results is particularly desirable to the plaintiff, a mediator can facilitate a resolution quicker, and on mutually acceptable terms.

Securities industry. In the past, disputes arising from transactions and activities in stock, bond and commodity futures trading were resolved with arbitration—neutral third parties deciding the outcome. Since most arbitrators were industry specialists, consumers began to question their neutrality. In addition, case loads caused backlogs of months or years. As a result, professionals in the industry are now calling upon mediation to resolve their conflicts. Using internal and external mediators as situations warrant, positive, constructive resolutions can emerge from conflicts that might arise among and between employees, brokers, brokerage firms and clients.

The Future of Mediation

As a mediator, I've watched the field expand into applications well beyond its traditional boundaries. Some of today's most widely used applications never existed, save for the imagination, not long ago: mediation in secondary schools, victim/offender mediation and mediating agreements in debt, divorce and business partnerships. All of these applications, inconceivable just ten to twenty years ago, are in widespread use today. This is a testimony of the versatility of the mediation process. I like to think that people are becoming more civilized, less vindictive. It could be the optimist in me, but why else would mediation spread so rapidly and into so many corners of society's angst?

As an industry watcher, I am in awe when I look at the new ground that mediation has broken over the last decade. Then I look at the unbroken ground that mediation has yet to plow, ground well suited to be turned another way should there exist mediators who see beyond conventional boundaries. In nearly every aspect of human interaction in which conflict impedes progress, mediation can meet a need. In this final discussion. I would like to look ahead to fields that mediation has not yet plowed, yet are perfect places for it to lessen the natural friction of human interaction and cultivate harmony. It is my hope that these fields will be areas that, in ten years, function more smoothly because of the impact of inventive mediators who thought enough to bring new plows into old fields.

Real estate transactions

Suppose you are buying a house through a trusted real estate agent from someone you never met. It's the house you and your spouse have been looking for for years. The location is close to the school your children attend; there are extra bedrooms for your guests and your home office; the roof is new; the plumbing is sound; the kitchen is bright and spacious; and it has something you've always wanted but never had the time to build: a trophy case. And it's a beauty, too—ornate, hand-carved mahogany with scrolled corners, stained glass and spot lighting. It would be perfect for your collection of Elvis memorabilia, even the tumblers, and suddenly you realize that you must have it, house and all. You make a pathetically low offer, which everyone does (or at least should do), and are surprised when the sellers accept. After you kick yourself for not making your pathetically low offer an *insulting,* pathetically low offer, you sign the purchase agreement. You are enthralled and begin to change your lifestyle to one that alternates between packing and jumping through all the hoops that home buyers have to jump through before the closing. These hoops include things like title searches, surveys, loan applications, credit references, termite inspections, septic inspections, plumbing inspections, inspections of the inspections and finally the appraisal, which is usually the most traumatic hoop of all. That's when you find out your pathetically low offer is ten thousand dollars more than the house is worth even if it were located on the French Riviera. They call this the "burst bubble" syndrome. It happens to every home buyer during the hoop-jumping phase of home ownership.

Fortunately, you get the satisfaction of watching someone else jump through the same hoops you are: the geek who made you a pathetically low offer for your home, which you had to accept at an embarrassing loss because it was either that or the joy of having two mortgages. This is possible only because the seller wouldn't agree that the purchase of your new home be contingent on the sale of your old home. He's played this game before.

Nevertheless, both sales proceed through the hoops. Three days before the closing you make a most disheartening discovery: the seller has removed the trophy case. You come to find out that it was a free standing case the seller had built into the wall to *appear* permanent. You scramble for your purchase agreement and scour it to see if the seller listed it as an exclusion. He didn't. You call the real estate agent and scream that the sale is off if the trophy case is not reinstalled before closing. The real estate agent investigates and calls you back with the bad news: the seller insists that the trophy case was not a permanent fixture and never intended for it to be part of the sale.

The entire transaction is on the verge of falling apart, making everyone losers in the fiasco. You threaten to sue for your deposit; the seller threatens to sue for the balance; and the real estate agent is on the verge of losing a tidy commission. It appears there will be no winners should this scenario continue to deteriorate. Furthermore, the entire transaction could take months to move through the legal system if allowed to progress in this direction. In the meanwhile, you have three weeks to vacate your home before the new owners take possession. This is what's called a "pickle."

Lucky for you, the real estate agent has been trained in dispute mediation. Faced with closing on your own home and with no new home to move into, you become desperate. Your real estate agent senses the impending loss of the sale and makes an offer to mediate a resolution. You both understand and accept the concept and agree to meet the day before the closing is supposed to transpire.

The real estate agent sets the ground rules, you both exchange facts, questions, and feelings and explore resolutions. The seller insists on taking the trophy case, being a family heirloom, but concedes to install another. You concede the antique and agree to his offer to install another. The real estate agent writes up the agreement, you both sign it, the sale proceeds, and you close the next day with no hard feelings, no lawyer's fees and no scrambling for some other place to live. The seller keeps his heirloom and salvages the sale, while the real estate agent collects the commission. Everyone wins because the real estate agent was skilled in mediation.

Mediation is perfect for real estate transactions that go sour and threaten to dissolve. With mediation the seller can keep the buyer, the buyers can keep their new found home, and the real estate agent can keep the commission—all with less expense, time, and anxiety.

There's a certain momentum that accelerates when buyers and sellers proceed toward a closing. Most buyers and sellers want their transactions to proceed to conclusion and are willing to make concessions in the event of a misunderstanding. Therefore, derailing the process takes a great deal of conviction. That's why removing the barriers to the sale is easier than for them to remain in place. But if real estate agents don't have the tools to remove the barricades, a sale will often be lost.

Mediation is on the cusp of this application. Several real estate agents are exploring the potential of incorporating mediation into their training sessions, and I suspect the results will justify the means. As you can see, when a sale that would be otherwise lost is recaptured and successfully closed because mediation preserved the momentum, that technique holds promise for the industry. Since mediation can be the difference between closing a sale or losing it, the spread of mediation into the real estate industry nationwide should only be a matter of time.

Prenuptial agreements

Another emerging application of mediation is in facilitating prenuptial agreements between couples who bring monetary or material wealth into a marriage or have the potential to inherit monetary or material wealth. With the divorce rate hovering near 50% percent (higher for second and third marriages), certain situations merit the protection of existing or potential assets from being part of potential divorce settlements.

For example, let's say you are in line to inherit the family business. It's an engineering firm your parents built to prominence from scratch and has become the exclusive engineering firm for all the franchises of a national frozen banana chain. The years of labor that your parents have invested are finally paying off and they are about to take the company public. At thirty-five years of age, you have just graduated with an MBA and immediately move into an upper-level management position with your parents' firm. Life looks pretty good, especially since your wedding to the heir apparent of another engineering company—the one that's been lusting after the same frozen banana chain's contract for years—is set for next month.

You both are bringing a good bit of potential wealth into the union in the form of future business ownerships. That's why both families have good reason to be nervous about your marriage. Should it fail, a greedy grab for each other's company may ensue that could put both firms in great peril. Even though you and your fiance are intimately dedicated to a life of blissful coexistence, your respective families are privately urging you both to establish prenuptial agreements that assure you can't grab for each other's corporate interests should the marriage fail—not an unreasonable request considering the potential devastation to each company should divorce rear its ugly head months or years hence.

A mediator would be able to facilitate an agreement between the betrothed to protect the interests, possessions, wealth and potential inheritances that they bring into the marriage. There may not be an actual conflict to mediate in such cases so much as there is a willingness to mediate an agreement to prevent a future conflict. Call it conflict insurance; call it conflict prevention; call it whatever you wish, but it's a perfect example of an application of mediation that holds great promise.

In cases such as these, it's a good bet that the families are more concerned about the marriage failing than the couple. More than likely, the betrothed understand the concerns of each family and are willing to create a prenuptial agreement that they themselves may not think is necessary, but don't mind establishing for the sake of their families' interests. The presence of a mediator guarantees the orchestration of the process by a neutral third party, an element that brings assurances to the families that fairness will override attempts to bias the agreement or further personal agendas. A mediator can also work to assure that the pending marriage does not collapse from the pressure of two attorneys entering into adversarial gamesmanship.

Individuals often bring financial or material wealth into a marriage that they have an interest in protecting—a house, a boat, a family heirloom, a vehicle or a substantial sum of money. It's simpler than mediating an agreement in which both families have interests at stake, but not much. These types of resolutions precipitate readily because of the high level of cooperation the parties bring to the session. The beauty of mediation is that *no matter who wants a resolution, the process is the same.* A mediator facilitates a prenuptial agreement with the same rules, the same premise and the same spirit of cooperation as if mediating a caustic conflict. For prenuptials, the approach is the same; only the degree of congeniality is different.

This prenuptial application is exactly why I am so optimistic about the future of mediation. When a device that was originally designed to help resolve conflict after the fact evolves into a device that can also *prevent* conflict, then that process has found its cutting edge. To be on that edge and to help that wonderful process create inroads towards a more peaceful coexistence in whatever ways it finds is an emotional high unlike any other. As mediation proceeds into the next millennium, new applications will inevitably be explored. These are exciting times. With every new field that mediation plows, newer fields emerge. Only good will come of it all. I am encouraged that you now possess the tools of mediation and have taken the time to be a cultivator for the greater good. It speaks well of you.

APPENDIX I

Consent and Confidentiality Agreement

We agree to enter into mediation in an effort to find a mutually agreeable solution to our dispute. We realize that mediation is a voluntary process and that no solution may be forced upon us. We further agree to refrain from attempting to use what is said by another during the mediation session in any further grievance or court hearing, nor will we attempt to subpoena notes, records, documents or persons from this session into any court or grievance hearings concerning the matter(s) currently involved in mediation. The termination of mediation is defined as when all parties have exited the building.

Signed,

DATE: /   /

APPENDIX II

Items of Agreement

Name:
Date: / /
Name:

In order to settle our dispute, we agree:
( ) To refrain from all verbal and physical abuse with each other.
( ) To refrain from the use of weapons of any sort against each other.
( ) To refrain from threatening or provoking the other to the above.
( ) To refrain from harassing each other in any way.
( ) To refrain from making harassing phone calls to each other.
( ) To refrain from going on the other's property without permission.
( ) If problems arise in the future, we will first try to work them out directly between ourselves. If we cannot, we will contact.
( ) As long as this agreement is upheld, we will not seek criminal or civil penalties against each other over incidents occurring prior to today's date.

Appendix III

Neighborhood dispute

AGREEMENT

In order to resolve our dispute, we agree that:

1) We will equally share the cost of one repair of Frank's mower not to exceed $60 each.
2) Frank is to supply Helen with a copy of the receipt for the parts needed.
3) Frank agrees to have Helen's leaves picked up by this Sunday evening.
4) Frank agrees to continue to remove Helen's leaves for three seasons. Helen will then be responsible for raking the leaves thereafter. Should Frank's mower break down again, Helen agrees not to seek a refund of her share of the repair bill.
5) Should Frank's mower break down during the duration of this agreement, he agrees to help Helen rake her leaves until this agreement expires.
6) Helen will be solely responsible for her own chiropractic bills.
7) Frank agrees to resume his willingness to be Helen's mechanic.
8) Helen may continue to use apples from Frank's tree and will supply Frank with two pies per year for the duration of this agreement.
9) If future disagreements arise, we will first try to work them out directly between ourselves. If we cannot, we will feel free to ask (mediator's name) to mediate between us again.

Signed_____
 Frank "Motorhead" Colucci

Signed_____
 Helen "Pies Я Us" Lumbago

Date   /   /

APPENDIX

Work place dispute

AGREEMENT

In order to resolve our dispute and be able to work together cooperatively, we agree that:

1) We will limit our personal calls during work and will ask those who regularly call us to limit their calls to emergency and very important calls only. We will request of our callers to defer all other calls of lesser urgency until we can take them at home.

2) We will pass all phone messages to each other.

3) We will continue to share our work load equally.

4) If problems arise in the future, we will first try to work them out directly between ourselves. If we cannot, we will feel free to ask (*mediator's name*) to mediate between us again.

Signed_____
                      Lucia Ramone

Signed_____
                Hernandez Cornucopia

Date   /   /

APPENDIX IV
Resources

(Compliments of the Community Mediation Association)

**American Bar Association
Standing Committee on
Dispute Resolution**
1800 M St. NW, Suite 200-S
Washington, DC 20036
(202) 331-2258
Information on ADR and the Courts; ADR legislation in the works or passed; good source of info for lawyers who want to get into the field.

**For ABA publications, contact:
Order Fulfillment
American Bar Association**
750 Lake Shore Drive
Chicago, IL 60611
(312) 988-5555

American Arbitration Association
140 W. 51st St.
New York, NY 10020-1203
(212) 484-4000
Information on arbitration of all types. They sponsor many conferences throughout the year.

**Association of Family and Conciliation Courts
c/o National Center for State Courts**
300 Newport Ave.
Williamsburg, VA 23185
(804) 253-2000
Information on court-based family and divorce mediation and arbitration.

Federal Mediation and Conciliation Service
2100 K St., NW
Washington, DC 20427
(202) 653-5290
Information on labor disputes.

Mediation First
101 Crescent Ave.
Louisville, KY 40106
(502) 897-3020
Fax: (502) 897-1545
Commercial, Personnel, Divorce, Custody mediation services, and mediation training.

APPENDIX

Mennonite Conciliation Services
21 South 12th St.
Akron, PA 17501
(717) 859-1151
Early developer of mediation services. Many written resources.

National Association for Mediation in Education
1726 M Street, NW, Suite 500
Washington, DC 20036-4502
(202) 466-4764
Information on teaching dispute resolution skills and mediation training for students. Annual conference.

National Institute for Dispute Resolution *(Same address and phone as above) Provides workshops and institutes, technical assistance, project development, research and evaluation in the field.*

National VORP Resource Center
c/o **St. Vincent de Paul Center**
777 S. Main, Suite 200
Orange, CA 92668
(714) 836-8100
Information on victim-offender mediation/reconciliation programs.

Society of Professionals in Dispute Resolution
100 Connecticut Ave., NW
Suite 700
Washington, DC 20036
(202) 833-2188
Membership organization. Information on the dispute resolution field, referrals to practitioners. Conference every two years.

U.S. Institute of Peace
1550 M St., NW, Suite 700
Washington, DC 20005
(202) 457-1700
Grantmaker which funds peace research and conflict resolution studies. Focus is on international conflict.

Teacher Training and Graduate Programs in Conflict Resolution

Below is a relatively comprehensive list of graduate education programs in Conflict Resolution and/or Peace Studies.

Conflict Resolution Certificate Program
The University of Phoenix
Center for Professional Education,
Management Development Center
4615 East Elwood Street,
2nd Floor
Phoenix, AZ 85040

Graduate Program In Conflict Resolution California State University
Dominquez Hills
P.O. Box 43784
Los Angeles, CA 90043
(310) 516-3770
Internet: 6500dew@ucsbuxa.bitnet

Institute for Dispute Resolution Pepperdine University Law School
(Graduate Certificate and Master's Degree)
Malibu, CA 90265
(310) 456-4655

Center on Conflict and Negotiation Stanford University
Crown Quadrangle
Stanford, CA 04305
(415) 723-2696

Institute on Global Conflict & Cooperation University of California
(All Campuses)
9500 Oilman Drive
LA Jolla, CA 92093
(619) 534-3352

ADR Certificate Program University of Denver
2000 South Gaylord Way
Denver, CO 80208-0295
Program on Conflict Resolution
University of Hawaii
(Master's Degree in Conflict Resolution, Mediation, and Peacemaking)
Department of Political Science
242 Maile Way, 717 Porteus
Honolulu, HI 96822
(808) 936-8984

APPENDIX

**Dispute Resolution
Certificate Program
Boise State University**
Continuing Education
1910 University Drive, L- 1 04
Boise, ID 83723
(800) 632-6386 ext. 1709 in Idaho
(800) 824-7017
 ext. 1709 outside Idaho

**Martin Institute for Peace
Studies and Conflict Resolution**
University of Idaho, I 0 1 -XOO I
Moscow, ID 83843
(208) 885-6327

**Peace Studies Program
Associated Mennonite
Biblical Seminaries**
3003 Benham Avenue
Elkhart, IN 46314

**Graduate School of
International Studies
University of Denver**
School of International Studies
Denver, CO 80208
(303) 871-2989 x2539

**Social Conflict Program
University of Colorado at
Boulder** Department of Sociology
Box 327
Boulder, CO 80309
(303) 492-6427

**Peace & Conflict Resolution
Studies American University**
School of International Service
Washington, DC 20016
(202) 855-1522

**Mediation Institute
Nova Southeastern University**
(Graduate Certificate, Masters, and Ph.D.) School of Social and Systemic Studies 3301 College Avenue
Fort LAuderdale, FL 33314
(800) 541-6682 x5708
Internet:
 warters@alpha.acast.nova.edu

**Conflict Resolution Program
The Carter Center
Emory University**
One Copenhill
Atlanta, GA 30307

**Peace & World Security Studies
(PAWSS)
Hampshire College**
West Street
Amherst, MA 01002
(413) 582-5321

Program on Negotiation
313 Pound Harvard Law School
Cambridge, MA 02138
(617) 493-1684

**Social Economy and
Social Justice
Boston College**
Department of Sociology McOwin
Fall 426 Chestnut Hill, MA 02167
(617) 552-4130

**Peaceable Schools Center
Lesley College**
154 Auburn Street
Cambridge, MA 02139
(617) 349-8405

**Degree Program in
Dispute Resolution**
(219) 295-3726

**Institute for Peace Studies
University of Notre Dame**
P.O. Box 639
Notre Dame, IN 46536
(219) 239-2970

Loyola College
(Certificate in Conflict
Resolution and Certificate in
Prevention of Youth Violence)
4301 N. Charles Street
Baltimore, MD 21210

**Dispute Resolution Institute
Hamline University Law School**
1536 Hewitt Avenue
St. Paul, NM 55104-1284
(612) 641-2068

**Conflict and Change Center
University of Minnesota**
(Minor in Conflict Management)
(612) 625-3046

**Dispute Resolution
Program University of Missouri
(St. Louis)**
Department of Sociology
8801 Natural Bridge Road
St. Louis, MO 63121
(314) 553-6364

**Negotiation & Conflict
Resolution Center
Rutgers University**
15 Washington Street
Newark, NJ 07102
(201) 648-5048

**International Center
for Cooperation and
Conflict Resolution
Columbia University,
Teacher's College**
Box 171
New York, NY 10027
(212) 678-3274

APPENDIX

Peace Studies Program
Cornell University
1800 Uris Hall
Ithaca, NY 14853
(607) 255-6434/6370

Center on Violence and
Human Survival
John Jay College of Criminal
Justice City University of
New York
New York, NY 100 1 9
(212) 237-8431
A.A. White Dispute
Resolution Institute
University of Houston
College of Business
Administration 325 Meicher Hall
Houston, TX 77204-6283
(713) 743-4933
Fax: (713) 743-4934

University of Massachusetts,
Boston
100 Morrissey Blvd.
Boston, MA 02125-3393
(617) 287-7421
Internet:
  krajewski@umbsky.cc.umb.edu

Peace and Conflict Studies
Wayne State University
3229 Cass Avenue, Room lot
Detroit, MI 48202
(313) 377-3433

New York City Consortium
New York University
East Building, Room 635
239 Greene Street
New York, NY 10003
(212) 998-3494

Analysis & Resolution of
Conflicts Syracuse University
(Certificate, Master's, and Ph.D.)
410 Maxwell Hall
Syracuse, NY 13244
(315) 443-2367

Program in Nonviolent
Conflict & Change
Syracuse University
Maxwell School of Citizenship
& Public Affairs
305 Sims Hall
Syracuse, NY 13244
(315) 443-3780

The Conflict Resolution Center
University of North Dakota
(Continuing Education)
P.O. lox 8009, University Station
Grand Forks, ND 58202
(701) 777-3664

APPENDIX

**Conflict Resolution Program
Antioch University**
(Master of Arts in
Conflict Resolution)
800 Livermore Stecet
Yellow Springs, OH 45387
(513) 767-6321
Internet: mlang@igc.apc.org

**Graduate Program in
Sociology of Conflict
Bowling Green State University**
Department of Sociology
Bowling Green, OH 43403
(419) 372-2294

**The Justice institute of
British Columbia**
4180 West Fourth Avenue
Vancouver, British Columbia
Canada V63 4VI
(604) 660-1 875

**Alternative Dispute Resolution
Program University of Utah**
(Graduate Certificate Program)
Department of Communication
7400 Language & Communication
Bldg. Salt Lake City, UT 84112
(801) 581-7648

Woodbury College
(Graduate Certificate, Associate's
Degree) 6600 Elm Street
Montpelier, VT 05602
(800) 639-6039 or (802) 229-0516

**Inst. for Conflict Analysis and
Resolution George Mason
University** (Master of Science
and Ph.D.)
4400 University Drive
Fairfax, VA 22030-4444
(703) 993-1300
Internet: mboland@gmu.edu

**Institute for Conflict Studies
and Peacebuilding
Eastern Mennonite University**
Harrisonburg, VA 22801-7462
703-4324450

**CORPUS Program
Seattle University**
Theological and Religious Studies
Seattle, WA 98122
(800) 426-7123

University of Victoria
Begbie Building
P.O. Box 2400
Victoria, British Columbia
Canada V8W 3H7
(604) 721-8777
Fax: (604) 721-6607